SHIFT ON

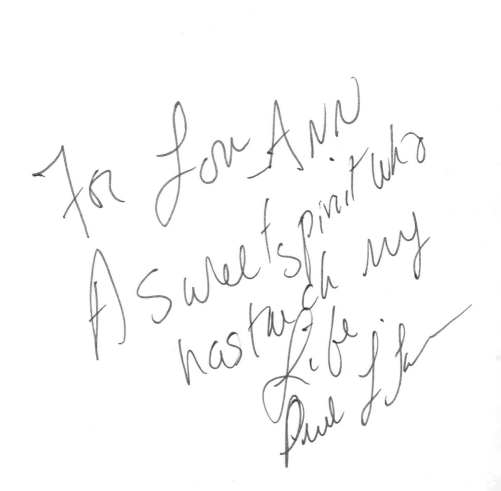

For LouAnn
A sweet spirit who
has touch my
Life
Paul Liba

SHIFT
ON

Twenty Stories of Turning Trials into Triumph!

NIKKI WOODS

ISBN-10: 0-9962513-1-6
ISBN-13: 978-0-9962513-1-0

Library of Congress Control number: 2016901108

TABLE OF CONTENTS

INTRODUCTION

Dear Friend,

Imagine freezing your life in this place and time and being able to truly assess where you are, who you're with, and how you're feeling physically, mentally, and spiritually. Obviously we can't do that. We are in a constant state of motion, even when we make an attempt to be still long enough to listen to the inner voice that sometimes directs our actions.

When we are intentional about doing what is needed to make our lives whole we have to shift forward.

In 2014, I had a vision for collaborating with other women who had stories to share about how they succeeded against the odds. What started out as a book turned into a movement when women and men got a taste of the kind of freedom such honesty and introspection can bring.

In "Shift On: Twenty Stories of Turning Trials into Triumph!" authors tell how an intentional move has led to transformations in their relationships, jobs, spirituality, and their physical and emotional health.

As they share stories of divorce, chronic illness, death of loved ones, financial instability, and recovery, readers will walk away with practical tools for coping, healing, and pushing forward despite the challenge.

Each of the co-authors is committed to your success, so we have made Shift On interactive! In order to get free training videos, access to more resources, and free gifts visit http://shifton-thebook.com/bonuses. You'll not only get the tools you need for when roadblocks get in your way, you will get free gifts from some of the authors too! We also have a Shift community just waiting to support you! You can access that by going to https://www.facebook.com/groups/ShiftTheBook/.

After reading this book, you will be ready to take your own personal journey that will pave the way for your moment of self-discovery. The Shift is Real.

Shift on!

Best,
Nikki Woods

P.S. Shift doesn't happen in a vacuum. My heart is grateful for Necie Black, Mary Flowers Boyce, Ebony Combs, Aprille Franks-Hunt, and the many Shift Agents who stood beside me (and put up with me) through the creation of this movement. It will not be forgotten.

PREFACE

The 90s was *my* decade. It's the period when many significant things in my life took place. I went to college, I taught school in Jamaica, I began working in radio, and I was single, living life.

Back then, many of us were slaves to designer labels like Cross Colors, Rocawear, and FUBU. Even though I was fashionable I made it a point back then not to be too trendy, and I still do. Fashion trends come and go. I'd rather invest in a solid, stylish look that I really love than throw my money away chasing a look that will be out of style as soon as the next fad comes along.

I don't like lifestyle labels either. "Me Generation," "millenniums," "post-baby boomers," etc., are categories that make it easier for people to make us part of classes and cliques that we have no control over. And even though I'm a member or affiliated with a few groups whose causes I'm passionate about, I've never joined a sorority or a professional service organization and my boys have never been a member of a Scout Troop.

We are not anti-social, but I would say we're more pro-independent. I discovered a long time ago that there are ways for us to do everything we want to without having bi-laws and membership fees. Part of the reason I am a non-conformist of sorts is because I'm often more interested in the people who exist outside of the circle than those who are within.

Like most people, my family, home, and community have shaped my ideas.

I grew up in a middle class suburb, in a middle class family, with a father who left for work every morning with a briefcase, and a mother who at one time was the school nurse where my older sister and I attended. She later became a stay-at-home mom. My father was our protector and provider, my mom our caretaker.

While I did benefit greatly from having a solid upbringing from God-fearing parents, my life today for my children couldn't be more different than the one I had. I am a divorcee, raising two boys on my own. We are the family that I couldn't imagine being part of when I was growing up. But different isn't wrong.

When we left Chicago to begin a new life in Dallas, I had a choice to make. Faced with the reality that my boys would be raised away from their father, grandparents, aunts, uncles, and cousins, I could either fall apart or I could pull myself together and create the best life for them I possibly could.

I chose the latter.

Unlike my parents, who presented an almost-perfect life that has been difficult for my sister or me to replicate, my boys have seen the good, the bad, and the not so pretty side of being raised in a single-parent home.

When they were younger, I was enough. I was all they knew and probably all they needed. But as they get older, my eldest son especially, questions why we have been dealt the cards we have, why our life is not as traditional as some of his schoolmates, and whether it will ever be the kind of "normal" that lines up with what he sees in his head.

I am not only a single parent, I am a professional with a challenging, sometimes high-pressure job that I love as producer of a nationally syndicated radio show and the CEO of a media company I've built from the ground up. I leave for work while my boys are still asleep, I travel at least once a month, and while their father and grandparents are certainly apart of their lives, for all intents and purposes the roles they would play in a "normal" family have been parceled out among a village of people carefully selected, sometimes by trial and error. And so their circle of support has included at various times, a driver, a nanny, tutors, and most recently, a school management coach. I don't incorporate these people into our lives because I can afford to pay them to do something I should be doing; I incorporate them into our lives because they are what we need for *our* normal.

Like my oldest son, we can all weigh ourselves down at some point or another wondering if who we are and what we have is as good as or better than our friends, neighbors, co-workers, and even strangers. What I want my sons to know is that comparisons are a complete waste of time and energy. It's as unproductive as driving down a road looking through the side view mirror concerned only about who is coming near or passing us up or how close we are to crossing over into someone else's lane. Using this unsafe method of driving, we're sure to collide with the person in front of us at some point.

I'm teaching my boys, my coaching clients, and anyone in my circle to choose life and not labels. What you're called has very little to do with who you are and how you will live your life. Just as me growing up in a two-parent home didn't guarantee that for my children, my oldest son needs to be assured that him growing up in a single parent home doesn't mean that is what's in store for his future. My shift in thinking is to stop thinking about what could have been or will be and to concentrate on what is, and for my children to do the same.

It's all about the heart and hearts of the people we allow to be part of our lives. The impetus for the Shift Movement began with a spirit of collaboration and inclusion that much of the world frowns upon. The idea of men and women who have been left outside of the circle creating their own sphere of support is frightening to some. People would rather you think there's some mystical, magical way to get past the gatekeepers that have traditionally told us who could enter the sacred arena of writing, publishing books, songs, and movies.

Guess what? It's all a big lie.

The Co-Authors of "Shift On: Twenty Stories of Turning Trials into Triumph!" are examples of government workers, medical professionals, public servants, pastors, bakers, soldiers, and computer programmers who have been told "no" in their professional and personal lives and refused to allow a closed door to keep them out.

"Shift On: Twenty Stories of Turning Trials into Triumph!" is a chance for us to give a voice to those who would ordinarily not be given a seat at the table. Pull up a chair.

There's room for everyone. As we share ideas, resources, and platforms we become more open and more empowered.

Live *your* life, dream *your* dream, tell *your* stories. Shift On!

UNFORESEEN: LIGHTER SIDES

BY PRISCILLA L. JONES

"It is during our darkest moments that we must focus to see the light."

—Aristotle Onassis

"Whoa! This kid is white!" Doctor Kendrick shouted. I remember thinking, *Nah, everybody knows that African Americans babies are born a little light.* I saw her for a split second before the doctor rushed my newborn to the sink. My husband, Robby (aka Robert), in medical scrubs and the staff were ready to give Robyn her first bath. I heard my husband jokingly sing out, *"Oh Deeaar,* we've got to talk!"

It was 1988 when my labor pains began after I attended my first Secretary's Day Luncheon. That's right. I vowed that even though the delivery date was any day now, I would attend the luncheon. My prayer was answered. Just like clockwork, I received my usual dill pickle and joke for the day from one of my bosses. We laughed and then *Ta Dah…* labor pains! If you want to see even the strongest man show weakness, just tell him you are in labor; the expressions are priceless.

I made arrangements with my best friend, Lenora, for my daughter, Cameshia, to go to her home after school and spend the night with Lenora's daughter. Thankfully, the military base housing where we lived was close to my job. My husband was a medical assistant at the military hospital on base so it was a win-win situation. I was delivering at my husband's workplace. I decided I was going to make him proud, deliver naturally, and be very dignified with my pain. While walking to my hospital room, nurses asked me repeatedly if I still planned to deliver by natural childbirth. Feeling annoyed, but keeping my poise, the answer was always "YES!" But then I had begun to wonder if I really was going through with it.

The head nurse had a mean poker face that seemed to give me a sharp and painful contraction every time she came into the room. I was adamant about making a good impression, but the sharper the pains, the less polite I became.

Finally, after six hours of labor, the doctor arrived at 12:35 A.M., just in time to catch my baby in his hands. He seemed baffled because of her unusual skin color as if wondering, *"How can two brown-complexioned African Americans create a blonde haired, blue-eyed white child?"* He explained that my daughter was not maintaining her temperature and he needed to put her under the Bili lights (*a type of light therapy used to treat newborns' jaundice*) before I could hold her.

The nurses returned me to my room and I could not help but worry. Before Robby's night shift in the emergency room, he stopped by to check on me. He bought a Mrs. Baird's Apple pie that I craved throughout my pregnancy. He said he knew they were not flowers but it was all he could get from the hospital vending machine. My heart was touched that he was so thoughtful. He leaned over and kissed me on my cheek, whispering that I did a good job. Sensing my concern, he assured me that our baby was okay, and he explained the Bili lights. We named her Robyn—like Robby. Her middle name would be Clara after his mother who had died of cancer. We professed our love for each other, sealed it with a hug and a kiss before he left.

Meanwhile, I kept hearing Robby's co-workers walking down the hallway whispering, "Poor Bobby..." as he is known to them. Concerned, I decided to ease out of bed around 2:30 A.M. to see my little bundle of joy. Walking slowly with my heart pounding, I approached the nursery window. My eyes widened to see that all the babies were white, including mine! My eyes rested on Robyn sleeping under the Bili lights, with white hair and skin like a porcelain doll. I thought to myself, *She looks like an angel.* I saw one Vietnamese baby with dark hair and a less white complexion. I figured out what the whispers were about. I still hadn't told my parents. There was so much commotion in the delivery room and I wasn't sure what I would tell them. Finally, I returned to my room and called my parents in Virginia with the good news about our baby being born healthy and beautiful, and she looks like an angel. I did not mention the phenomenal circumstances surrounding us. Unable to sleep, I sent up a prayer of thanks for my family. Hours later my husband, and a doctor who flew in from San Antonio, walked in with a handful of papers. The doctor said cheerfully, "Congratulations! You have given birth to an Albino child!" My response, "Thank God, there is a medical term for this. I knew I had been a good girl!" Despite assumptions and whispers that I must have had an affair with the milkman or even my boss, my husband remained loyal and trusting in me—he did not waiver. I had carried this child for nine months, sight unseen, loving and praying she would have all of her fingers and toes…prayer answered. On the same token, I was just as shocked as everyone else to see her white skin, white hair, and blue eyes.

The doctor explained the ratio for Albinism was about 1 to 1000 and each parent must carry the gene. Albinism simply meant the skin pigmentation did not develop. Formally defined, it is *a congenital disorder characterized by the complete or partial absence of pigment in the skin, hair, and eyes due to absence defect of tyrosinase, a copper-containing enzyme involved in the production of melanin.* He explained that in order to determine whether our daughter was Tyrosinase positive or Tyrosinase negative, we need to wait to see if color develops in her hair and/or her skin because there are no tests. He explained the Tyrosinase positive Albino will probably outlive us all but, Tyrosinase negative Albino lifespan is only about seven years. An Albino's vision, at best, would be visual impairment or Legally Blind. We were given referrals to an optometrist and dermatologist. We became well-versed explaining Albinism from consults with dermatologists and the literature the doctor gave us.

In our despair, we sent up a prayer. Geneticists allude to the fact because each parent must possess the rare gene means the parents are blood related to produce an Albino. Wow! We did not see that coming. Go figure that I may have married my cousin; after all, I am adopted. My quest became to expedite research on my medical and social history as soon as possible. I called my friend, Lenora, trying to describe the circumstances. She was prayerful and thrilled. She said that she could not wait to see and hold Robyn when she brings Cameshia to meet her baby sister. I wondered if she heard me and concluded she'd see when she visited.

The next day two co-workers came by the hospital to visit. I led them to the nursery. They assumed the Vietnamese child was my baby. I pointed out Robyn. "Come on P.J., we know you are a practical joker but where is your baby?" They were still in disbelief until the nurse brought my infant daughter to my room. This was the first of many times I would explain Albinism. They both said they couldn't wait to tell my boss, Bob Harrod, that my baby looked just like him. Bob was white with blonde hair and blue eyes. Coincidence? You bet! Bob visited later, bearing a beautiful basket of flowers from my co-workers. Standoffish and uncomfortable, he implied he had never visited an employee in the hospital, but had heard about the baby. They won't stop teasing him so he came to see for himself. It was feeding time when the nurse brought Robyn into my room. Bob took one look and was speechless. He sighed, sniffed, then responded, "Oh, I see what they mean," and he left.

Saturday evening, Cameshia, rushed in with Lenora and a big smile seeing her baby sister lying in a bassinet. I knew she would be the only one to think nothing unusual about her little sister.

The previous summer, Cameshia asked if she could have a baby sister. I explained that we would have to ask her daddy. She then asked, "Momma, can she be white?" I laughed and explained,

"Well, now we REALLY need to ask him because mommy and daddy cannot have white children." Go figure, from the eyes of a child with 20/20 vision. Cameshia acts as if we had merely granted her a Christmas wish. Lenora said she knew a family in Mississippi with Albinism. She held Robyn saying, "Oh, look at her pretty blonde hair. I cannot wait to braid it!" We both laughed. I took a deep breath knowing there will be some difficult days ahead.

I enrolled Robyn in a nursery and returned back to work. The nursery staff was amazed and it took them some getting use to seeing Robyn. One day I was in a hurry to pick up Robyn and I saw all of the infants lined up in their seats in the nursery except Robyn. I asked the daycare attendant where she was. She gave me a puzzled look and said, "She is right there." All of the babies were white and I was thinking brown skin on that day.

Because she was so pale, any scratch or blemish on Robyn created suspicion to the public eye, especially at the nursery. Heartbreak ensued on one occasion when I had to leave work to explain to the nursery staff that the dark mark on Robyn's forehead was my goodbye kiss from wearing Black Orchid lipstick. I showed them the lip color. From that day on, I kissed Robyn goodbye before applying lipstick.

This was a different addition to our family and required much modification in everyday living. We had to learn how to locate the best shade and the different levels of sunscreen to apply on her skin. We had to be aware of whether it was sunshine or cloudy because her skin could burn easily. We had to purchase wide-brim bonnets to protect her delicate eyes from the sun. We had to adjust to long stares, whispers, and rude assumptions in public. Curious children did not hesitate to ask if Robyn belonged to us. I wondered how I would explain to our Albino daughter she was really our child since I was the one who was adopted. We could protect her from the sunrays, but how did we protect her from humiliation?

Shortly before Robyn's second birthday, she stopped laughing, responding to her name, and interacting with us. The day I dreaded of having to explain to Robyn why her skin color was lighter than ours, would never be an issue. Our beautiful babbling joyous Gerber baby became very quiet—almost without expression. We could not determine why she constantly banged her head against things on purpose. Was she in pain or was it frustration because we could not fulfill her needs? Our concerns led to the Pediatrician recommending referrals for hearing tests that yielded normal results but her behavior was growing more bizarre. We had to "Robyn-proof" our house, which meant latch locks on all cabinets, windows, and doors especially to the laundry room. Robyn had a tendency to hide in the dryer and under cabinets.

Robyn did not talk. We would search for her in panic mode because she would not answer when we called her; we were not aware she was playing hide and seek. Everywhere we went, we had to be aware of all window blinds because Robyn thought that was the best toy. Later, we realized due to her eyesight, the contrast in light stimulated her. As a toddler, Robyn was leaving a path of destruction. Sleep was not an option. We already noticed her ability to destroy window blinds, climb onto countertops and then on top of refrigerators. The first time I got her down from atop the refrigerator, I knew we had to seek help.

The military base doctors initiated testing for Tourette Syndrome (*neurological disorder characterized by repetitive, stereotyped, involuntary movements and vocalizations with tics*). They sent a video of Robyn we filmed on her first birthday party at McDonalds to Baylor College. Their assessment yielded negative results with a recommendation we take blood tests for Fragile X Syndrome (*a genetic condition that causes intellectual disability, behavioral and learning challenges*). Before we consented, Robby and I received counseling. The compassionate doctor said couples have divorced after the blood tests revealed the child's paternity, indicating a different father than on record. I had no doubt and nothing to hide, and Robby did not flinch. The tests were negative for the syndrome and because they automatically test for paternity the results were positive; Robby was the daddy.

Dr. Morton, Behavior Specialist, felt Robyn was too young to be put through a battery of neurological exams for Frey's Syndrome, *a rare neurological disorder.* He did not feel this was the reason for her behavior. The Family Advocacy referred us to Mental Health Mental Retardation (MHMR) who referred us to a Psychiatric Institute professing she was too young to make a diagnosis but it appeared her behaviors were that of Autism. We were like, "What? Another 'A' thing!" We understood Albinism. What the heck was Autism? *Autism is a serious developmental disorder that impairs the ability to communicate and interact.* Here we go. Another journey. I was fearful of the unknown but at least had a term to describe Robyn's unusual behavior. So how do we fix it? Our prayer list was getting longer while church attendance was diminishing.

The Psychiatrist at Woods Institute diagnosed our daughter as extremely Autistic and that we should not waste our time. He recommended we go ahead and commit her. He stated that children diagnosed with Autism have "refrigerator mothers," a term used to define an assumption that autism was caused by emotionally distant or cold parents. I was devastated. "Refrigerator mom" sounded judgmental and totally in conflict with whom I was. I considered myself as loving and caring not cold-hearted and unfeeling. The psychiatrist said that an Autistic child would never acknowledge our presence and were unwilling to form relationships. They lived in their own worlds. In a matter fact kind of way he said, "Ninety-nine percent of the time, parents realize that the situation is never going to get better and they waste their time trying to raise the child when it is better to place them in an institution."

I stood and as I politely removed our child from off the top of his desk, I said, "Doctor, you know that one percent that we have left? We are counting on that!" This was the day I learned how to stretch out on my faith!

Robyn displayed behaviors like none ever seen. Persuading her to wear clothes without protest was like pulling teeth. She preferred to wear the same thing every day. She preferred to eat the same thing every day. It was difficult to introduce change. She was not open to any deviation of the schedule or there would be major meltdowns. We could not determine which was the culprit to her behavior, the Albinism or the Autism.

Dangling objects, like beads and strings, fascinated Robyn. When we found out that playing with stringed objects held her attention and made her stay put, we became very creative. We invented "Stim Toys" a straw with a piece of yarn hanging from it or Mardi Gras beads cut in a single strand, both economical and easy to carry anyplace, and kept her entertained for hours. As long as she could repeatedly dangle those beads, we could go places without her trying to escape, conquer, or destroy.

We became well educated about Autism by attending support groups, conferences, and seminars as much as we could afford. The funny thing was we kept running into five of the nine families whose children were born on the same day at the hospital as Robyn. Those families were experiencing difficulties, challenges, and behaviors considered to be autistic tendencies too. Sleep deprivation was a common thread among all of us parents because children with Autism just did not sleep.

Robyn would play (bang) on the piano in the middle of the night and one of us would be up to applaud and stand guard to prevent any escape attempts. Lenora provided respite on the weekends so that we could have a sleep date—yes, we both actually went to sleep; the true meaning of sleeping together. Doctors suggested medication but we refused to experiment with prescription drugs for fear it would cause seizures—a side effect we did not care to risk. We decided to use Vitamin Therapy instead.

There were times when we had to do things just a little different than most families. We figured out ways to coax Robyn to listen and obey. Cameshia shared techniques from her Elementary School Speech Therapy class with us to use with Robyn because Robyn flapped her hands to get our attention. Cameshia was able to reach her little sister with sounds and gestures. We learned some sign language. We noticed how Robyn responded to clapping hands so we used one loud clap as a sign of, "No." Applause was a sign of approval. Singing was how we let her know there was change of events so she would not get so frustrated. Our Psalms for living: song for going to school, song for bathing, song for church—we had a song for everything.

By the time we drove from Texas to Virginia to spend Christmas with our hometown folks to see our newest family member, 18-month old Robyn, we were exhausted. We sent pictures with attempts to explain all we knew about Albinism, and preparing ourselves for comments. We were surprised to find out how many relatives and friends including my mother had seen or knew an Albino from our area. However, Robyn's desire to climb reached a whole new height when my father nodded off in the kitchen. The next thing you know, Robyn was jumping up and down on top of the kitchen table. My daddy was startled awake yelling for my mom and me to come and get her. Robyn's behavior was "shock and awe" with some fear for my parents. My husband's side of the family was more accepting as they knew several Albino families.

My husband and I were used to the gawking stares and whispers but we did believe it took its toll on Cameshia emotionally. She began having problems in school and difficulty making friends. Cameshia loved her sister but at eight years old, she was a little embarrassed during a "Robyn episode" and hid her face or tugged at my shirttail crying, "People are looking at us!" Cameshia was always a very sensitive child. Eventually we realized Cameshia had communication and learning challenges diagnosed Attention Deficit Hyperactive Disorder (ADHD). We sought therapy, Ritalin prescribed, and an Individual Education Plan for her.

I thought, *God has a sense of humor.* Laughter was God's little commercial break when we're stressed in darkness and not able to see the lighter sides of things. I was thankful for the gift of humor and it went right along with patience. One day I noticed Robyn standing in the fish tank with the goldfish swimming around her little legs. I put the laundry basket down and asked Robyn if she was pursuing scuba diving or did she just need to take a bath. I would rather laugh than cry—or are they the same emotion?

Daycare services were difficult to obtain because of Robyn's behavior and potty issues. The phone calls from the daycare to pick Robyn up were everyday. I resigned from my job to take care of my baby girl and was a stay-at-home mom for a brief three weeks, when unbeknownst to us, Robyn started Early Childhood Intervention which allowed me to return to the workforce. Apparently, the change for her to go was in the works but not communicated to us that it would happen as quick as it occurred. Robyn's classroom was named "The Autism Room." You could walk in and see children running rampant, disrobing, screaming, and crying. I was devastated! We did not know we would become advocates but I thought, *The curriculum MUST CHANGE!* I fought to have the room name changed at an Admission, Review, and Dismissal (ARD) meeting where my husband and I brainstormed with the ARD committee. We agreed to STARS (Special Techniques are Reaching Students).

We thought Robyn was a late-bloomer so talking and attending school would resolve the problem. Communication challenges and sheer frustration in the classroom setting confirmed that Robyn was developmentally delayed nonverbal (*not involving or using words or speech*). Living with a nonverbal person who is Autistic was like playing the game Charades 24-7. We had to assume different types of roles and be like mimes, learn gestures, create sign-language to communicate with our daughter. She had to be prompted and coached into simple activities that we all took for granted like dress, potty, sit, eat, and many daily routines which were challenges for Robyn. Our love for music helped to reach her since speech and language function were in different parts of the brain than music.

I feared losing my new job because of the lack of afterschool and summer care services for special needs persons. My outcry (with real tears) to Robyn's caseworkers promoted action to explore the State School in collaboration with MHMR (Mental Health Mental Retardation). Both agencies were willing to implement a trial, as this had not been done before. We devised a plan including Robyn's strengths—music (piano), Swim Therapy, and obtained a Foster Grandparent to read, sing, and sit in the swing with her. The

Caregiver position was developed with the main requirements being that you must love Robyn. Lenora was the only person who fit the job description. She moved from San Antonio to fill the position.

While serving on committee boards and making proposals to recognize the need to implement Daycare and Afterschool Special Needs program, we recruited Nonprofit organizations including Texas Division for the Blind, MHMR, the State School, Special Education Teachers, friends, and families like us. I also had great emotional support from co-workers; after all, I was employed with Children Protective Services.

We paved the way for Robyn and other children with challenges. By the time MHMR launched daycare services in an old school building for Children with Special Needs, Robyn was school-aged, too old to utilize the services yet they honored us at the Grand Opening.

We were placed on a waiting list for Home Community Services to assists families who decided to keep their disabled child at home rather than institutionalize them (Robyn, at six, years was the youngest). Care for any child can be expensive but a child with special needs can be very expensive. We bought pull-ups, mattresses, and bed linen more often than most. Robyn qualified for Supplemental Insurance Income (SSI) from Social Security but based on our family's income she was ineligible to receive monetary benefits.

Doctor Morton from San Antonio, who was also instrumental in educating us on Autism, heard about our family's plight. He recommended a place Robyn could go for one week each summer to give us a break and would help with teaching Robyn routine daily living skills. CAMP Camp (Children's Association for Maximum Potential) in Center Point, Texas (developed by military doctors and nurses for pediatric patients with special needs). I was reluctant because Robyn was still nonverbal with multiple challenges. I was protective and careful not to place her at risk for abuse. Cameshia trained as a volunteer to keep a watchful eye and that was the best thing we could have ever done as CAMP helped resolve Robyn's enuresis. Robyn has not missed a summer yet.

We are Family! My mom is 92-years-old and still living in Virginia in the same house that my late father, Alphonzo, built. Our family demographics now—35 years married; we are grandparents to beautiful, college-bound, 15-year-old Shenise, whose mom, Cameshia, is an awesome 34-year-old single parent. Robyn, our 27-year-old special needs, adult daughter, lives next door in a Person-Designed apartment that we converted from a three-car garage. I had to pretend I did not have a paycheck for a year, along with subsidies from a resource helped to fund the apartment project. Lenora introduced us to a compassionate contractor, Donnie Perry, and we got the job done just in time for Robyn's graduation present in 2010. Do you remember that 1%? It equals FAITH.

"The way I see it," my cousin Marion leans forward to express with much affection, "God has issued each one of us a map for our life, and it is up to us to follow His Plan." Those were the most comforting words anyone ever spoke to me at what felt like the darkest time in my life. Words of wisdom can shed light. When the road gets a little rough and I am not sure where my map of life is leading me, I can always rely upon one of the most precious gifts the Lord has given me—PRAYER! You can find answers and blessings when you learn to pray. Thank you Elizabeth Virginia Peyton, my momma, for teaching me how to pray (to *offer spiritual petition, devout praise or request to a supreme being higher than self*). When we say Grace to bless our food, the one word Robyn is able to say clearly without prompting is "AMEN."

Our journey in life leads us on unpaved highways, crooked byways, sharp turns and curbs, one-way streets with potholes, and dead ends. There will be detours in our personal identities, but under its construction is the core path and map of our true identities of self. Like the effects felt from the earthquake when I felt that shift in the earth under my feet, the title to C. Nathaniel Brown's book cleverly states it all, "SHIFT HAPPENS THEN YOU LIVE."

Chalk it up to memories and to love. Love is a feeling but it is also an action. Being busy with as many challenges as we have can wreak havoc on a relationship and you start to take each other for granted. When that happens, stop and examine your heart—take self-inventory. The power of love can make you happy but it can also make you cry. A good soul cleansing can help you regain focus especially when your life is under construction. Everyone has a map planned by God, which details the route to good events; you just need to follow the predetermined map by God with faith. Sometimes, we resist following the good and we take detours, which may lead to bad events.

Unexpected life-changing events present themselves and families and relationships are forever altered but at the root we were able to love and shift too. We draw and retrieve the immense knowledge from our soul that drives the personal identity, which exerts a powerful influence on our treatment of others with unforeseen lighter sides.

YOUR POWER IS IN YOUR THOUGHTS

BY BRITT YAP

"With everything that has happened to you, you can either feel sorry for yourself or treat what has happened as a gift. Everything is either an opportunity to grow or an obstacle to keep you from growing. You get to choose."

–Wayne Dyer

Growing Up

Ever since I was 10 years old, I enjoyed writing and knew I wanted to be a journalist. I loved telling other people's stories and I felt a deep sense of gratification when I would see my articles printed in my high school newspaper. I loved that each day was different, each story was different, and in each interview I learned something new. After high school, I received an academic scholarship from Hawaii Pacific University (HPU) where I went on to receive my B.A. in Journalism and M.A. in Communication. Throughout my college years, I was an intern for some of the biggest print newspapers in Hawaii and even worked as an intern at the Associated Press. I had also started my own mixed-martial arts magazine at 23 years old, and became one of the youngest college teachers when I was hired as an adjunct journalism instructor for five semesters at HPU. The University later went on to hire me full time as the assistant director of University Relations.

All my life I've been a go-getter. Constantly pushing my limits whether it be physically—playing soccer, basketball, softball, gymnastics, hula, and track and field—or in education—receiving scholarships for my grades and nominated in my bachelor's and master's degree for valedictorian. I never gave myself a break. In fact, I felt guilty when I wasn't doing something to further my schooling, sports, or career. A lot of it has to do with my upbringing. Both of my parents were coaches and excelled academically at whatever they set their minds to. Both were highly motivated and encouraged me to follow through on my commitments. My dad would say, "If you're going to do it, do it well. Or else, don't do it at all." My mom had high expectations for me when it came to my grades, and my dad when it came to sports. As the only child, I didn't want to let either of them down. I wanted to be the son my dad never had. So I tried every sport I could possibly sign up for. And I wanted to please my mom so I worked hard in school.

Living With A Chronic Illness

"You must take personal responsibility. You cannot change the circumstances, the seasons, or the wind, but you can change yourself. That is something you have charge of."

-Jim Rohn

I carried on this type A personality in high school and college. College was a lot like high school. I played soccer, wrote for the school newspaper, was involved in a few other extra-curricular activities, and volunteered in the community. I was like the energizer bunny that kept going. I felt guilty for taking a nap or a day off. Over time, this pressure I put on myself started to affect my health. I didn't realize it then, but my life was not in balance. All of my life I felt well, never seeing my doctor for anything more than a routine checkup and the occasional cold, so it never occurred to me that this pressure and high expectation was bad for me.

In college, and after months of being in severe pain with no answers as to why, doctors diagnosed me with ulcerative colitis (UC)—an inflammatory bowel disease (IBD) that causes long-lasting inflammation and ulcers (sores) in your digestive tract, affecting the innermost lining of your colon and rectum. There is currently no cure. A person who has UC is either in a flare up or remission. Symptoms vary depending on the severity of inflammation and where it occurs but the ones that I experienced on a regular basis was diarrhea, rectal bleeding, fatigue, fever, and abdominal pain. When I was in a flare up, I'd be running to the bathroom 30-40 times a day. And that's not an exaggeration. The urgency and unknowingness of having that feeling to go poop really does a number on you. It makes you paranoid and makes you want to stay home all day and be near a comfortable bathroom. While there is no factual evidence as to why people get UC, I know in my heart a lot of my condition was due to stress and me worrying about things I had no control over.

The next eight years were manageable for the most part. My symptoms were under control through the sporadic use of medications and I only had a few minor flare ups. These flare ups would last a couple months and were stark reminders that I wasn't superwoman anymore and I needed to take time off for my health and learn how to relax and say "no" sometimes. Most people don't understand how depressing this condition can be. It's not something that is easy to talk about with your family, friends, coworkers, or classmates. I appeared fine on the outside, so people assumed having UC was really not that bad. But inside it felt like my colon was on fire. I was completely embarrassed about my symptoms, and worst of all, when I left my house I was constantly worried if I'd make it to the bathroom in time. Imagine being in your 20s, in your dating prime, going to college, and having to explain to someone you crapped your pants. And although ulcerative colitis usually wasn't fatal, it was a serious disease that, in some cases, caused life-threatening complications.

Most of my stress came from relationships and pressures I put on myself to be the best I could be. Although ridiculous, I couldn't see it then. Society and my upbringing programmed me to be paranoid about success and working hard all the time. I wasn't taught enough about having balance and peace of mind. My Honors Literature professor gave me a book about meditation because she said I was too young to be having this type of health problems. I remember skimming through the book. It felt like a foreign language to me. *Meditate. What's that?* I thought, *I can't possibly quiet my mind and think about nothing. That's impossible.* After that, I didn't revisit the word meditation until many years later—when it became crucial to do so.

Then in November 2010, God answered my prayers. I met a man 'beyond my wildest dreams' when he was on vacation with a group of friends in Hawaii. Our eyes connected across a bar, he walked over and chatted with me, we exchanged numbers, and from that moment on, our souls have been inseparable. Although we'd just met, it felt as if we'd known each other for decades. Our values, our goals, our personalities; all just fit like a glove. We spent the next six days of his vacation hanging out, and before he went back to California we made a commitment to each other to give the relationship a try.

Rod and I decided we could no longer live apart. After both of us offered to quit our jobs and move for the other, I felt this was my opportunity to experience life somewhere new, so I quit my job, packed up my apartment, and moved to Alameda, California to start our life together. The first few months were exciting. Everything was new and I couldn't wait to find a job and settle into this new city. My UC was in remission and he knew about my condition and was extremely supportive. Whenever I didn't feel good, he was totally fine with us missing an event and just staying home to rest.

Your Power Is In Your Thoughts

"If you can change your mind, you can change your life."
–William James

I'm still not exactly sure what initiated the worst flare up of my life, but a lot of factors were in play—new job, new living situation, having to make new friends and create a support system away from Hawaii, and a killer 3-4 hour commute each day.

In March 2012, just three months into my new job at Santa Clara University, my UC symptoms started to come back and I was in a flare up again. I tried for a few months to work with my doctor and try different medications, but nothing seemed to be helping. In fact, some medications made my symptoms worse. My stomach felt the worst in the mornings and driving for two hours in traffic made me extremely paranoid because I worried I would have to use the bathroom while stuck in traffic. All the while, Rod, my rock, remained incredibly supportive.

Finally, one night Rod and I had a big talk about our future together as a family and what would be best for my health. We decided that it would be best for me to quit my job and by the end of the year move back to Hawaii. We believed this would help me get better. The work commute alone was killing my stomach and making me incredibly paranoid. We had to crunch the numbers and see if it was even possible to live off of his income, but somehow we vowed to make it work; even if it meant us selling two cars, a boat, and some other prized possessions. So in July, I resigned.

August proved to be the one of the most daunting months of my life. They say the hardest transitions in life are a death, a move, and a new job. Well, I was going through all three in one month. I found out a childhood friend of mine had suddenly passed away on August 5th, I took a job offer for a high stress position of office manager for a Hawaii state representative that was scheduled to start mid-August, I was trying to figure out logistics of moving us back to Hawaii—cost for shipping our cars, boxes, furniture, and find a new place to rent on Oahu—all the while being on a one-income budget and my health continuing to worsen from the stress.

Then one night in August, I came downstairs and Rod was in the kitchen cooking dinner. I sat at the dining room table and began to feel dizzy. My eyes rolled back, my breathing labored, and I blacked out for a minute. He rushed over to check on me and immediately decided to pack us up and rush over to the emergency room. Doctors told him it was a good thing he brought me in because my vital signs weren't so good. It was the scariest time in my life because I didn't know how to control anything anymore. My body felt as if it was shutting down. I was in so much pain that I'd often be screaming for the nurse to give me more pain medication. It was like my entire stomach, intestines, and colon were lit on fire and I had no control over my bowels.

For the first few days I couldn't eat solid foods. I was stuck to my bed, only having the strength to walk a few feet to the bathroom. My mom, Rod, his family, and our close friends came to visit me, trying to keep my spirits up. But most days I just felt tired, in pain, and out of control. What was plaguing me the most was I was supposed to start my new job in Hawaii that weekend, and I didn't know how to tell the boss that I wasn't going to be able to move back on time. Still, in all of this pain, I didn't have my head completely focused on healing. I was worried about my responsibilities like my job and my friend's funeral that I was missing. Friday, a few days after being in the hospital and no good news, doctors told me I needed surgery to have my colon completely removed. They brought in a surgeon to talk about the procedure, which they wanted to schedule right away. Because none of the medications were helping, this was all they could do for me. There would be a few more surgeries after the initial colostomy to reposition my intestines and connect it to my rectum.

The surgery did not sound fun and despite my mom and Rod encouraging me to do it, I had a feeling in my gut that I couldn't ignore. The feeling said that the colostomy wouldn't go well. I trusted my gut. Except for the nurse taking my vitals, I asked to be left alone for the weekend. I didn't want to speak to anyone about the surgery. I just needed my space. They obliged.

For the next two and a half days I focused. I got my mind right. I realized my power was in my thoughts. That was the moment when my first awakening or SHIFT happened and I thought to myself, *My mind got me in this mess, my mind can get me out of it.* I decided to pick up the phone and call the state representative I was supposed to work for and kindly tell her I had to decline the job offer. The minute I got off that phone call, as hard as it was to disappoint her, I felt a weight lift off of me: that responsibility now gone. Then I sent flowers to my friend's family because I felt immense guilt that I couldn't be there for his funeral. Once I took care of that, I felt another weight lift off of me. I decided now was the time my health had to come first. Nothing else mattered if I didn't have my health, or if I was dead. I finally got the lesson!

I spent the rest of the weekend focusing on visualizing a healthy body and a stress-free mind. It's amazing how your body responds to your thoughts. Positive thoughts can heal your body. I had strong visualizations of my colon being healthy and my mom did some energy healing (Reiki) on me. By Sunday, I was able to eat solid foods and walk around the hospital.

When Monday rolled around, the doctors were in shock of my vast improvement. My blood work improved and vital signs were stabilized. When asked what I did, I replied, "I realized my power is in my thoughts," and I smiled. A few days later the doctor decided to release me and let me go home and rest and see if I could continue improving. They also found a medication that started to work and help with my inflammation.

In the hospital, Rod was doing research online and he found that hypnotherapy could help people with UC. So as soon as we went home, he called a hypnotherapist with good reviews and scheduled four appointments for me. After just four sessions with the hypnotherapist and working on pain relief and stress relief, I was able to better handle when the pain came on and was in general more at peace in my mind. I became a huge believer in Reiki and hypnotherapy because it was two natural healing modalities that helped me tremendously in my healing process. I believed in it so much that I wanted to learn more about it and take classes.

Surrendering To My Purpose

"Take the first step in faith. You don't have to see the whole staircase, just take the first step."
-Martin Luther King, Jr.

Rod and I had been married for a year when we moved back to Oahu, Hawaii around October 2012. While my condition was improving, I still was in no way ready to take on a 9-5 job or sit in traffic commuting to work every day. I spent the majority of my day in bed resting, watching television, and contemplating what was next for me. And even though I was drastically better than I was months ago, I still had days that my colon would feel so sore and I would just poop blood. Looking for some answers in life about what I should do next, I looked up a psychic-medium in my area. I found a woman by the name of Yoshie Miakoda Chihara (later becoming my mentor and good friend) who had some good reviews. When I contacted her, I was hoping to hear from my grandpa who passed several years prior and my friend who had passed in August.

While I wasn't able to connect with my friend during this first session, I did hear from my grandfather. Yoshie gained my trust and I got a few messages from my grandfather that day. There were a lot of things Yoshie told me that only my grandfather and I would know. But the message that stood out the most came two minutes before I stood up to leave. Yoshie took a long pause, looking over to the left side of the room, and then looked back at me. "They never usually do this. Spirit does not intervene and tell someone what to do with his or her life. But in this case, spirit is giving me permission to tell you this. They said you will be a counselor of some sort, and you will help lots and lots and lots of people," said Yoshie.

I immediately rolled my eyes, chuckled, and said, "I'm not going back to college to get another degree in psychology or counseling. I'm done with school already."

She looked at me and grinned. "That's not what we mean. We just know that you are destined to help a lot of people. It doesn't mean you have to go back to college. It may be in the form of getting certified or taking other classes." And that's what she left me with. I couldn't stop thinking about that comment for the next two months, especially since I was already interested in learning more about hypnotherapy and Reiki.

Then right around Christmas, I had an incredibly rough night. In fact, it came after a few bad days where my UC symptoms were unmanageable. My husband and I were staying at my mom's house on Maui for the holidays. It was 2 A.M. and everyone in the house was asleep, except for me. It felt as if I was going to the bathroom twice every hour and I couldn't sleep at all. My colon felt like it was on fire. I wanted to poop, throw up, and cry all at the same time. I found myself whimpering in pain, hunched over as I sat on the toilet bowl, and tears began rolling down my face. I was tired. I was tired of this life. I was tired of being sick all the time and in so much pain. I said to myself, if I didn't have my husband and my parents, I would seriously just want to give up and die.

Then while I was sitting there, I started talking out loud, just sharing my frustrations with God: "*What do you want from me?*" I yelled. "*What have I done to deserve this? I know I have more that I'm destined for than this. There has got to be a bigger plan for me than to just sit at home all day, in pain, and be of no use to anyone.*"

And that's when my second awakening or SHIFT happened. If I was really, genuinely asking God to show me what He has in store, I need to surrender and trust His process and pay attention to the signs He's showing me. It was that early morning in Winter 2012 that I made a deal with Him.

"*If you get me at least half way better to where I can at least get out of bed every day and function without pain, I will do whatever it is you want me to do with my life. Whatever purpose you have for me, I will do,"* I told him.

I didn't realize how big that moment was for me until a year later. It was the second biggest shift I faced in this process of finding myself. In the months that followed, God was very clear that I should leave the 9-5 world and start my own healing business. Opportunities and the right people came into my life at the right time. I remained open-minded to the process and going with the flow. For the first time, I didn't know where I was going, but I wasn't afraid. I knew He was guiding me.

People oftentimes stop from taking the leap they desperately need to take because they haven't figured out the HOW. You don't have to know exactly how your goal is going to happen. You just have to know what you want and then take the first step. The rest of the process will start to reveal itself, but you need to do your part in having the courage to take the first step.

Helping Others Heal and Progress

"A life best lived is a life by design. Not by accident, and not by just walking through the day careening from wall to wall and managing to survive. That's okay. But if you can start giving your life dimensions and design and color and objectives and purpose, the results can be staggering."

-Jim Rohn

When I was a kid, and even in my adult years, the question, "What superpower would you like to have?" came up from time to time. My answer was always the same. "I want to be able to heal people so they don't have to suffer." Most of my friends would answer with flying, being invisible, and creating money from nothing. Little did I know all this time that I was speaking this healing thing into existence.

I spent the majority of 2013 starting up my business. I got certified as a life and business coach, hypnotherapist, and Reiki

II practitioner. I practiced working on friends and family and got feedback on how to hold my sessions. I continued to have reaffirming signs and dreams letting me know that I was on the right path. In fact, my business name 'Holomua Healing Arts' came to me in a dream. In Hawaiian, Holomua means "to improve; to progress." It fits perfectly because my mission was to help people heal and progress in their life.

Each day, I continue to be grateful for each one of my clients and I trust that God is bringing us together for a reason. He believes I can help them. Over the years I learned that you must have a plan, but be able to adjust your plan according to what life throws at you. For example, like a ship sailing off to sea. You have a plan of how you'll go about getting to your destination. However, if the winds change or a storm pops up, you have to be able to adjust your sails, go on a different course, but still be able to get to your destination.

Here are a few truths or habits I've learned to live by:

1. Be in alignment by always honoring your truth. Like Gandhi said, "Happiness is when what you think, what you say, and what you do are in harmony."

2. Start your day off thinking about three things you are grateful for and do a 15-30 minute morning meditation to help you clear your mind and be present.

3. Block out or avoid the jealous and/or negative people in your life, and choose to surround yourself with people who believe in you and are vibrating at your level.

4. Be different. It's okay. You don't have to conform to society or be a sheep. Go ahead, be a wolf. Or heck, be a possum. Do whatever fits you and your goals and purpose in life.

5. Learn how to have detached compassion. Master this and you'll never carry someone else's burdens.

6. The Law of Attraction—it exists and it's extremely powerful once you figure out how to use it to your advantage. Don't worry about things. You're actually doing more harm to yourself by actively attracting what you don't want to happen to you.

7. Time is more valuable than money. You can always get more money, but you can never get more time. (So stop worrying, you're wasting time.)

8. Have mentors and people you look up to. Study what they do, how they do it, and what makes them so successful. Then apply what you can to your life.

9. Nothing can replace hard work. You must put in the time and the sweat in order to reach your goals to be successful. "Success is neither magical nor mysterious. Success is the natural consequence of consistently applying the basic fundamentals," says Jim Rohn. So create good habits and do them daily.

10. Give Back. You don't have to be rich in order to start doing that. It's important that you help others in need and get behind a few organizations or missions you believe in and donate your time, money, and/or expertise.

While I grew up in the Catholic religion, I consider myself more spiritual than anything else. I have a strong, direct relationship with God and I talk to Him every day. I believe in energy, I believe in mindfulness and being present in the moment, and I believe in coming from a place of love rather than a place of fear. My journey has brought me to a place of having an open mind and open heart.

Some of the most compassionate people are usually the ones that have been through the worst things in life. They don't judge, they just listen and lend advice when asked. They are open, loving, and helpful. They've been there before and have chosen to bounce back and appreciate life each and every day, not taking it for granted. I am incredibly grateful for the trials, tribulations, and joys experienced early on in my life to get me to this place where I know my life's purpose and I'm living it each day.

Finally, don't compare your life to anyone else's. We are put on Earth as individuals, each with our own purpose. We are not all the same nor meant to have the same experiences, talents, or blessings. Once you stop comparing yourself to others and start embracing your passions and purpose, the universe will respond and your life will progress in amazing ways. Understand that you aren't a victim. Things aren't happening to you, they are happening FOR you. The universe is always working in your favor, you just have to trust it and change your way of thinking.

SHIFTING ON PURPOSE

BY DR. JENNIFER HOBSON, ABD

"To be who you are and to become the very best that you can be is the only goal worth living."

–Alvin Ailey

My mother is talented, smart, and the success story of our family. She taught me everything about being a confident, successful black woman.

She taught me etiquette, like how to sit, talk, and walk. She also gave me the initial tools that I could use in my career, like how to hold a conversation, shake a hand, be professional, get a job, and most importantly to chase my dreams.

Having danced since the age of two and taught dance at the Dallas Black Dance Academy since the age of 11, my dream was to dance professionally, but my mom made a point to educate me on the average income of a professional dancer—$17,000 a year. My mom made a point to enlighten me on how to monetize my dancing profession by going behind the camera, teaching, choreographing, in addition to being a professional dancer.

My mother taught me that as a black woman, I had to get my education, and that no one could ever take away my mind; they could take away my job, or my ability to dance, but never my mind. She mastered those words of wisdom through the difficulty of facing racism while growing up in the 50's and 60's. She engrained in my mind that I could do and be anyone I wanted to be. With that, I was tasked with one thing: to go to school and do well. So I started thinking about becoming a dance teacher, the choreographer, the studio owner, the producer, or the director, looking far beyond being just a dancer. Success was not an option—it was expected.

I attended Booker T. Washington High School for the Performing and Visual Arts as a dance major, received five full dance scholarships from renowned university dance departments, and was accepted to the school of my dreams—Spelman College. Although I was elated to receive my acceptance and scholarship award letter, it was really no surprise because Momma told me I could do anything if I worked hard enough. However, two weeks before I was scheduled to move into my dorm, my scholarship was recounted due to lack of funding, and my mother could not afford the annual parent loan. With discontentment in my heart, I was forced to attend University of Texas in Austin as a Presidential Scholar in Dance.

Of all of the things I had learned, I didn't know how to stay focused once I had a taste of freedom. I didn't know how to recognize the signs when a man was not good for me. I missed the chapter on loving self and not settling. I also missed the chapter that told me that my goods were more precious than diamonds and deserved to be worked for. In hindsight, not having a father around and not having some important conversations, it is no shock that I became a victim of abuse.

So It Begins

Just turning 18, I started college and within months I was dating. I was actually dating a Kappa who was a Christian and went to church. He was doing well in his classes and treated me well. He studied with me and took me on dates to eat and for ice cream. However, I was attracted to an older "lighter" type, so I dumped a person that was wonderful, for a person I knew nothing about because he seemed more established. Truthfully, he was fine. He was tall, slender, light skinned, had a great smile, and could dance his butt off, twirling his Crimson and Crème cane. He, too, was a Kappa and the Step-Master of his Frat, a leader, and I was attracted to that.

Naïve, I believed everything he told me. He said he was a senior, had a job, a car, and his own apartment. I thought I'd found someone like me—an achiever.

In my third month of college, I was kicked out of my dorm for being "black". I lived in an off-campus private dorm and I was one of a hand-full of minorities living there. When I was told I had no right to be there, I called my mother crying hysterically while students screamed and banged on my door. My floor mates said they had not paid their money to have a black girl in their dorm. I was terrified. I called the front desk and they said there was nothing they could do so my mom called the police. The police came, escorted me off the premises in safety, and told me to go stay with a friend and come back in a couple of days. I called my boyfriend, and he "rescued" me from the situation. I was numb. I had never experienced racism before. I only knew the stories my mom had shared.

I could not see my way out and I had no idea what to do. I was in a new city, had no real friends, and I was scared. I went back to my dorm room three days later and all of my clothes, bedding, family heirlooms—everything I brought from home—was gone. The police made a report but did nothing. I went back to my boyfriend's house and he said I could stay with him. Instead of going to class or seeking counseling, I depended on him; he became my savior. When I started living with him, I was absent from classes for about three weeks. I was too embarrassed to tell my professors what was going on. I was devastated, depressed, and drowned myself in my boyfriend's arms.

My mom came down and rented an apartment right behind my boyfriend's, which proved a horrible idea. I had come to depend on him as my savior, to tell the truth, and in my heart he could do no wrong. Yet, I began to see more things that alarmed me. Once, I was driving his car to a fraternity party with my friends, thinking

I had "arrived", when I found another woman's phone number in the ashtray. My curiosity was sparked, so I searched and found evidence of another woman whose name was also Jennifer. I found house keys and all sorts of things. So I was thinking, *Why is this stuff in his car when I'm his woman? Who is she and why you got her keys?* When I asked him about what I'd found, he lied and told me that it was "a friend's" stuff that she'd left when he gave her a ride home. Instead of trusting my gut, I gave him the benefit of the doubt. However, I kept catching him in lies. Often he would be without his car without explanation. He took secret phone calls, and I did not know what to do.

I started digging and found the other Jennifer's number in his phone so I called her. I introduced myself as his girlfriend and asked who she was. She explained that they were close as best friends, and she too had found my stuff in her car. Yes, HER car. She knew there was another woman "involved" and told me HE was lying to me and she was pregnant with HIS child. She let him take the car home every night and he picked her up every morning and took her to work—even going to doctors' visits together. I wondered, is this the kind of man I fell for? Did he deserve me? Because surely, if he did this to her, he would do this to me. Moreover, if he wasn't truthful about this, what else was he keeping from me?

I was furious. I did not understand why he would lie to me. When he came home, I confronted him and I was all up in his face. That was when the abuse started. He was 5'11" an athlete, and muscular; I was 5'4" and barely 140 lbs. I had no chance against him. He grabbed me hard and pushed me away from him onto the couch. Stupidly, I followed him throughout the apartment and would not let him leave because I needed answers. Then he threw me on the floor and left.

I cried for hours. I was too ashamed to leave him and I was too ashamed to go home. True to my nature, I had to "fix it" and make it work. I did not know at the time I was pregnant. He came back home later that night with the car, telling me the car was his, that he loved me, and that we were going to be together. Again, I gave him the benefit of the doubt and stayed.

When I missed my period, I made an appointment at the University Clinic and he took me in for a pregnancy test. Sure enough, I was pregnant. Feeling like a statistic—young, unmarried, and pregnant—I was ashamed but I took comfort that my boyfriend was a "senior" soon to graduate, or so I thought, and figured he would take care of us. I thought I would take off a year from school and go back after I had the baby. That was the plan in my mind. We received the call from the nurse confirming I was pregnant, while he coached his little league basketball team. He acted excited and gave me a hug. He took me back to his apartment and immediately left to go tell his mother the "good news." When he didn't return, I was devastated. Everything began to unravel in my mind. I was pregnant, another woman was pregnant, and he left me alone all night. He did not answer his phone and in my heart, I knew he was with her. I rummaged through his apartment, looking in everything. It had not dawned on me that I never saw him go to class. When did he go to school? In my search, I found military discharge papers with his real age, his ex-wife's name, and their kids. The man had kids! He was 12 years older than I was, not the four he told me.

I was beyond furious. I was hurt. I was ashamed and filled with guilt.

When he got home the next morning, I confronted him. That was when he took his Kappa cane, that he displayed so proudly, off the wall and hit me for the first time. While on the floor, he continued to hit me. He even sat and pinned me down, put his hands around my neck, and squeezed. I do not know what made him release his grip, but he did. I knew at that point I needed to terminate my pregnancy. How was I to have a child of a man I did not know, who was in his 30s, with an ex-wife and kids, and had another woman pregnant? I had missed school, had not danced in weeks, and I had to get my life together.

I scheduled a termination and went to endure it alone. I cried the entire time, and for days afterward. I fell into a depression. I tried to drop my classes before getting F's, but arrived at the Dean's office 15 minutes too late. I had just found out the man I thought I loved was abusive, I killed my child, realized I was homeless, and I felt like I was without family or friends. I vowed never to tell anyone what I endured. For the first time of my life, I had not reached my goals and I was ashamed of myself. In my mind I hoped to make the relationship work out, so I went home for the holidays then went back to school, determined to finish the year and right my wrongs. I got my financial aid, had plans to pay my rent for the semester and stay away from him. But he called and asked for another chance and I said okay. He brought his kids to the apartment to introduce them to me, and I thought I was special because I'd met the kids but I only became the babysitter for weekends at a time. The day I cashed my Financial Aid check, we "made up" that night and I spent the night with him. I had all of my money in the back pocket of my jeans and when I woke up the next morning my money was gone; so was he.

All the money I needed to survive for my 2nd semester was gone and I was stuck. I still tried to make the relationship work, live with and forgive him, but the abuse continued daily—emotional, verbal, and physical. He was not attractive to me anymore and it was clear he did not love me, and I am not sure he ever did. I was depressed again from the termination and actually prayed for another baby. I thought the baby would fix him—fix us. I thought the baby would make him not be abusive. He said I was lying and did not believe I was ever pregnant. Instead, my second pregnancy ended in a miscarriage from the stress. Still, I stayed.

I found myself 18, being beaten with a cane, isolated without any money, strangled more times than I can count, and in a hopeless situation. I lost my scholarship in dance and almost flunked out of school, all in my freshman year.

One day I asked him to take me to campus because I wanted to leave, so I jumped in the car and demanded he take me. He drove behind the garage and slowed down, reached over my lap to open the door, and pushed me out.

"How had I gotten here?" I asked myself. How did I not see this coming? How had I lost my way? How did I lose myself? How did I fall for this man? My mother had taught me better. I asked myself, "Why me?" Most importantly, why was it so hard for me to leave? Then it hit me: Mom had taught me never to give up. I was now learning that giving up and making a mistake was not always bad. Pregnant for the 3rd time, I was determined to survive and carry my child to term; despite the shame and guilt I carried. I was thinking a little clearer at this point. I fought to stay in school after receiving three F's my first semester and finished the year with a 2.49 GPA. I called my mother and said, "I am ready to come home." After eight months of abuse, I decided I'd had enough.

I arrived back in Dallas after finishing the school year and although five months pregnant, I returned to teaching with the Dallas Black Dance Academy. I was offered an opportunity of a lifetime to dance in a Broadway Musical—Miles Davis Gershwin's Porgy and Bess choreographed by the Legendary Hope Clark. I danced with and next to legends in the field of modern dance, and no one ever knew I was pregnant.

My mother told me to never let anyone see me cry, and I didn't.

I was focused on dancing at my best and I worked hard and studied the script, intent in reclaiming my career. So much so, on opening night our director visited my dressing room. She brought gifts for everyone in the cast and gave me an African fertility pin. I still had not told anyone I was pregnant.

How do you explain that you left Dallas as a Presidential Scholar in Dance, a professional dancer, and successful dance teacher, only to return with your life in shambles? How do you share that you got pregnant out of wedlock, lost your scholarship, and your baby's father beat you? I was ever grateful that she did not share my secret, but instead gave me her blessing to have my child.

Shortly after, my mentor and dance "mother" who saw talent and potential in me at such a young age, told me that I was no longer a role model if I had my child. I had two choices: either give up my child or abort him, otherwise, I could no longer teach at that dance institution. I was crushed. I gave my life to the institution. I began dancing as a professional there at the age of 15. I taught hundreds of students and directed the student company. I gave them my life and in return, they turned their back on me when I needed them the most.

I found myself alone, literally, working full-time, attending community college for a year, and a new mother of a baby boy. The father followed me to Dallas, made a failed attempt to re-enter my life but ultimately refused to acknowledge he was abusive. Most importantly, he refused to get help. Therefore, I put myself into counseling. I found The Family Place, entered battered woman's counseling, and sought healing to understand what had happened to me. I learned the cycle of abuse, how abuse was learned, and the signs that I'd missed. I learned that my son would learn to be abusive if he was taught, and I had a duty—an obligation—to ensure that did not happen. I set out to do just that.

Abused Again

Without being fully healed, I was 21 years old and sought a husband and father for my son. I met and eloped with another abuser. I knew he was a cheat when I married him. I knew he watched porn and I thought because he had three children that he would be a good father for my son. We had a beautiful daughter together, and I was an instant mother of five. I did not know fathering children was not an automatic characteristic of a good father or husband. I believed every story he told me and I thought it was love.

The truth was I had no idea what marriage looked like, and again did not foresee that emotional, mental, physical, and sexual abuse was around the corner. I was called everything but a child of God. I was scratched, bruised, tossed, thrown, and pinned down often. My metal daybed was broken, him using my back as the tool bending it into pieces. I often interjected my body in between his belt and the naked bodies of my stepchildren. My children would come home, turn-on the TV to find a pornographic video playing. I even found magazines in my sons' room. I was forced to do sexual things that no woman should have to do just because her husband said so. Because of that abuse, I was rushed to the ER with internal bleeding, requiring emergency surgery. At the young age of 24, I lost half of my female organs making it extremely difficult to have more children; something I have always wanted to experience the right way.

I ran two businesses and raised a family of seven, my husband included. I sought counseling alone. I never called the police and I thought I could take it. I thought I had to endure—he was my husband. I thought that if I kept making the money, kept buying houses and cars, kept the family looking like we were perfect, the Reconciliation and Calm stages of the Cycle of Abuse would manifest and stay; they did not. I felt like I had a constant black cloud over me—following me. I gained 150 percent of my weight and was diagnosed with asthma. I was constantly sick and life was like living in hell.

I had three pastors and three Christian counselors tell me to leave. With the help of my then deacon and deaconess, one time I had the perfect escape planned. I left with my two children and started over in an apartment. The peace was too unfamiliar. Even though I left the man who abused me in every way, I felt bad because he needed me. How would he and the kids survive? So I let him come back and my mother was devastated. All of those around me were devastated. No one could make me leave or make me see I was dying daily. All they could do was wait until I had enough, and be ready to catch me when I really left.

That day came in 2009. I guess God said, "Daughter, you haven't been listening. I have sent you help. I have heard your prayers but you are not listening. That's okay, because I am going to force you to." Boy did He ever.

My son told me that my husband was abusing him and *that* I could not accept. Two days later, I left. It was done. It was over. I left everything. My children and I walked out of that house with two small backpacks filled with their favorite books and toys, and one suitcase of clothes. I left my businesses, the house, two cars, all furniture, and all belongings. I left with nothing, yet I had everything. My husband cleared out my business account, forced my studio to close, attempted to kidnap my kids, and did everything humanly possible to try to force me to come back; typical of an abuser. However, when a woman is done, a woman is done. I got myself into that mess by not consulting God, but He was a faithful God and provided a way out. His grace and mercy were sufficient.

The Shift Begins

I began a new level of healing in 2009 to understand how I walked into an abusive relationship twice and not see it coming. I entered counseling again and began to learn how God made His plans for me. I regrouped. I owned my hurt, pain, and humiliation. I learned about my unhealthy patterns and the lack in my life, and what I was overcompensating for. I learned how to love myself, and how to love my children as they healed. But, I also acknowledged the enemy's schemes against me. I devoted years to learning how the enemy comes to kill, steal, and destroy in our lives and the tools he uses in his attacks.

I studied marriage; I studied how God made man and woman. I even had to look at myself and learn mistakes I'd made, and own them through self-confrontation. It was difficult and we struggled. I applied for assistance, went to food banks, and learned to re-budget, to do without, and to reclaim my life. I let go of bad habits I'd learned during the marriage and abuse. We learned the real meaning of family all over again. I allowed myself to be divinely disciplined. I focused on God, my family, my business, and then me. I started the process to forgive and set healthy boundaries for my family and myself. Ultimately, I learned that God had a purpose for everything and that not all that I had gone through was for me. It was for someone else and maybe more than one somebody. God wanted to use my story to heal other women.

I went back to school, ended up getting a third master's degree, and then began doctoral work. I have over seven years' experience as an academic scholar and professor at some of the best universities in the state of Texas. At one point, I was working three jobs, teaching at a non-profit educational organization and teaching at two colleges. I did what I had to do.

I moved my children into a house and gave them a stable life. I showed my kids that you could bounce back from anything with God on your side. I showed my daughter that it was not how hard you fall; it was how you choose to get up. I demonstrated to my son why it was important to respect his sister and the women in his life. I surrounded my son with positive role models, and I was honest and transparent with my children about what they and I had experienced. That came with a lot of anger, pain, heartache, and confusion; but I hung on for the ride and demonstrated what real love looked like. I taught them to love, respect, and set healthy boundaries for themselves. I taught them to run and chase after their dreams, and never stop.

Today, my daughter is the owner of her own company and an intern for a celebrity Emmy Award winning Interior Decorator. She has been written up in the newspaper as an up-and-coming entrepreneur. My son is an aspiring college basketball player, award winning track-star, and Sergeant in the MCROTC program. He is a talented videographer and dancer. These accomplishments did not come without hard work, tears, frustration, and a ton of prayer and faith. However, it all started with a decision to shift the direction of my life. It started with the decision to make a phone call, to pack three bags, to seek counseling… it started with my decision to start over.

It was the hardest decision that I have ever made in my life—to shift into restart; to start over again. Nevertheless, one I would gladly make again. Today, I speak and advocate for Domestic Abuse Awareness. Today, I volunteer and give my time to women in abuse shelters and fleeing from abusive relationships. In 2014, my company produced our first annual "I'm A Survivor" Symposium benefitting survivors of abuse from two organizations devoted to the fight against domestic abuse. In this, I found my calling. In this, I found my true purpose. In this, I found that I am so much stronger and I am happier for it. I am no longer a victim or survivor of abuse.

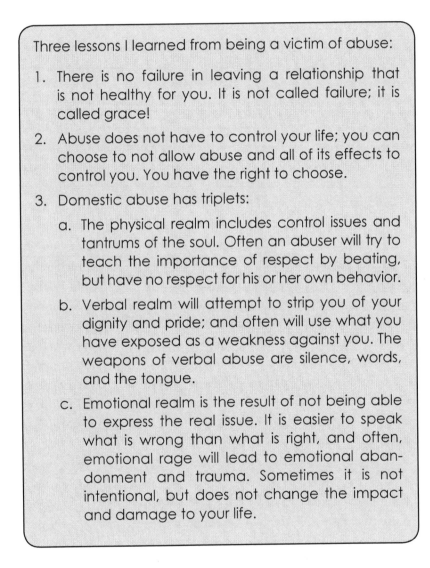

Three lessons I learned from being a victim of abuse:

1. There is no failure in leaving a relationship that is not healthy for you. It is not called failure; it is called grace!

2. Abuse does not have to control your life; you can choose to not allow abuse and all of its effects to control you. You have the right to choose.

3. Domestic abuse has triplets:

   a. The physical realm includes control issues and tantrums of the soul. Often an abuser will try to teach the importance of respect by beating, but have no respect for his or her own behavior.

   b. Verbal realm will attempt to strip you of your dignity and pride; and often will use what you have exposed as a weakness against you. The weapons of verbal abuse are silence, words, and the tongue.

   c. Emotional realm is the result of not being able to express the real issue. It is easier to speak what is wrong than what is right, and often, emotional rage will lead to emotional abandonment and trauma. Sometimes it is not intentional, but does not change the impact and damage to your life.

My lessons to you: educate yourself on the triplets of abuse so that you can empower yourself and take care of you. No women deserves or can ever force anyone to abuse her, however as women we do have control over what and who we allow in our lives. People can only do to us what we allow them. Know this: you cannot know where you are going until you know where you have been. Knowing where you have been will change the direction you are going if you will submit to the process.

The Blessing in Disguise

I can look back now and say confidently that everything I went through, that was meant for my bad, was used by God for my good. And for that, I am ever thankful. I was not aware that others were depending on me to survive, to shift into survivor. At The Family Place, they realized with my experience, that I needed someone who would be tough on me, if I was going to survive what and who had been placed in my life. So, they gave me the best they had; and boy, was she tough—but she was real. She demanded that I open my eyes. She helped me face my fear. She stood next to me as I admitted the abuse I received. She was instrumental in my life. She counseled me for years. I will never forget her.

One day in 2013, I had to call the counseling center to request some documentation. I was told to leave a message for her. Unsure if she would remember me, I left her a message and she called back immediately. My eyes filled with tears when I heard her voice. It was amazing hearing the person that coached me through the most difficult times of my life. She remembered me; every detail. We laughed. We talked. She assisted me with my need and we disconnected. I sat and I cried immediately after the call as I looked over my life. However, the phone rang again. She called back to say thank you, to let me know that she was glad that I'd called and to inform me that she was retiring from the business, after 20+ years of servicing women of abuse. I wondered how she did that, to face abuse day in and day out. I sat in amazement and wondered how she could be thanking me: she saved MY life. She told me that in her career, most women do not make it out: most women go back. She told me that it was a blessing to hear from me that day, as she prepared to retire, to know that one of her women, one of her girls, made it out. She told me that day that I was her success story. I froze. My heart stopped. I replayed over and over what she said in my mind, and I finally got it. I was alive. My kids were alive. I was a success story? I was her success story. I AM her success story! I shifted my life in the right direction. I will carry that with me everywhere I go. I am so much more than a survivor... now I'm an advocate.

SOME GIFTS COME WRAPPED IN SANDPAPER: *GETTING TO MY "NEXT"*

BY ERICA DANIEL

"The pain you feel today will be the strength you feel tomorrow."
                                                    –Unknown

I was at a critical crossroads after walking down a path that had been traveled by many. The resulting range of emotions was extreme as I experienced the closure to the final chapter of a 29-year marriage. I had experienced challenges in the past, but lying to rest a man who I had grown together with was different. Feelings of sadness, loss, and fear battled against an underlying peace, the peace from knowing the vast power of God. Leaning on that knowledge, I took one moment at a time as I went through the motions of funeral and burial planning. In the course of three months, my life changed, never to be the same again. This was not the plan. It was not supposed to happen this way. A whirlwind of thoughts ran through my head. Will I be able to be both father and mother to our children? Can I balance the stern hand a father brings, with the loving touch of a mother who adores her sons?

The morning began with great expectations of the night ahead. We were going to see Lady B herself—yes, Beyoncé. We looked forward to hanging out in the suite and enjoying drinks and conversation with friends. Every detail was covered, even down to the VIP parking. Shortly after leaving for work, my husband, Charlie, called and said his back was hurting and he was going to the emergency room to get checked out before the concert. I told him I was on my way and would meet him there. As I drove, I was thinking, *Okay, hubby is getting old. One too many golf swings and now he's pulled a muscle. It'll be fine.* We were placed in a room and Charlie explained how the pain was getting progressively worse. He explained that he had taken a fall the week before and also played several rounds of golf. Maybe the combination of the two caused his back to hurt. Charlie, being the guy he was, had the doctor laughing as he shared his story. The doctor said, "Well, let's be safe and do an MRI instead of an x-ray." While they carted him away to imaging, I opened my laptop in an effort to do some work. Upon his return we chatted about our pending plans and what we could get for lunch.

When the doctor returned, his smile was replaced with a wrinkled forehead. I thought it strange but did not give it a lot of weight. He went on to explain that the test results were back and they were not what he expected. He proceeded to say the screen reflected that Charlie had Lymphoma. As the word registered in my mind, I remember my anger rising. *Who are you, Mr. ER Doctor, to walk in this room and after one test, tell us we have cancer?* I felt like we had cancer because this man had been a part of my life for over 33 years. My love for him was unconditional. The more the doctor talked the more my insides began to cave.

My heart was so heavy as I fought back the tears. Tears that could not appear because if they had, it would mean I believed what the doctor was saying was true. I turned to my right and saw my husband's face. A face that needed to hear everything would be all right. I had nothing to give him. I prayed to myself, *God, I am going to have to draw my strength from you at this moment so I can give him the comfort he needs.* I stood and joined hands with my husband. If this was true, we were in this battle together. A night

with expectations of light conversation with friends and live entertainment was replaced with a nights stay in the hospital in which
we entered into deep conversation, connection, and prayer as we
awaited additional test results.

After several more tests, Charlie was diagnosed with Carcinoma
of unknown primary, CUP, a rare disease of the tissue that lines the
inner or outer surfaces of the body. The malignant cells are present
in the body, but the place the cancer originated is unknown. We
now had confirmation. It was during our three-month battle with
cancer that I saw God's provision first-hand. After seeing the power
of God time and time again, I became comfortable with expecting
the power of God. That expectation is what fueled me and allowed
me to maintain joy. There were many who did not understand why
I was not complaining or showing signs of defeat. They often said
I was so strong. This appearance of strength was just a byproduct
of my confidence in God's provisions and my expectation of his
power. You see, if it were not for that faith and expectation I would
have been useless at a time my husband needed me the most.

As reality had it, I shed many tears as Charlie slept. Many times
I was empty inside and fatigued. When I was at my breaking point,
God restored Charlie's health just enough for us to leave the hospi-
tal so I could go home and recharge.

Our Oncologist, Dr. Nguyen, was more like a family friend
than a doctor. This man was accessible 24/7. He gave us his cell
number and always answered when we called. We were at the hospital so often the staff became like family. They treated Charlie
more like a hotel guest than a patient. My manager at work was
more than supportive and openly offered his prayers of support. I
cannot begin to tell you how my family and extended family came
through. After three months, I found myself sitting on the front
pew, hearing the beautiful voices of those who are singing from
their hearts and the words of encouragements from those who had
grown to love Charlie. It was in those words that I received my
final message from my husband. That message was for me to stop
putting my dreams on lay-a-way.

In the midst of all the tears, he was there one final time to give me the nudge I needed. I felt liberated. It was in my greatest tragedy that I found a jewel representing a huge tipping point in my life. I could finally give myself permission to pursue my dream; a dream that started over 30 years ago when I was a freshman in college.

I was sitting on stage at an Awards Ceremony with this dynamic lady by the name of Patricia Russell. Just like every other freshman sitting in that assembly, I expected this dull, "You are adults now—be responsible," kind of speech. Instead I experienced the genius of a lady who by the end of her speech she had me feeling like my success was not an option but an obligation. I was ready to take on the world and pursue excellence with no regard to the color of my skin or my gender. I could feel her energy and I could see the response of the audience. I knew that one day I would be doing the same thing, helping others to embrace their potential and live life to its fullest. I wanted to be like her one day and have my words inspire others. That desire never went away and nudged at me as I continued my college experience.

At that time, I was 19 and was all about getting the grades that would allow me to keep my scholarships, get a good mentor, get me into the best sorority on campus, and pave my way into corporate America. I had a five-year plan that included graduating in four years and securing a job at a top software company.

The desire to inspire others was always in the background. I would be the first to encourage a person to pursue new opportunities. If you needed a personal cheerleader, I was your girl. I loved helping people dream big. But, I placed more priority on gaining my financial independence and making my parents proud than I did on that desire.

I entered Corporate America as planned and liked it. But I always found myself having those "one day" conversations with people. You know it goes like this, "One day, I will be a motivational speaker and life coach." By the time I looked up, my "one day" conversation had lasted for 25 years. All that time I simply placated this desire by mentoring, doing workshops, and speaking when asked. I let thoughts and expectations of what it took to be successful in corporate America, in effect, put my dream on lay-a-way. I aligned my priority more with the goals of family and career more than the goal of pursuing my passion, and it worked well for me up until this moment.

Reflecting on my final message—my final gift from Charlie resulted in a range of emotions. Feelings of affirmation and gratitude battled with a sudden sense of urgency and panic, as I embraced the realities of my own mortality. The desire to live in my purpose was like an erupting volcano in my spirit, and the question of, 'Why not now?' was like a song that was set on repeat in my head. I knew, that I knew, that I knew that all the obstacles and catalyst moments were there to prepare me to serve others. My journey had not been easy but it was rich in the blessings of insight, growth, and wisdom. Knowledge and experience that I can leverage to be a blessing to others by helping them realize their value and move into that next level in their personal and business lives.

That was my shift moment. It was time to end my 25-year-old "one day" conversation and replace it with a "today" conversation and boldly walk in my purpose. It was time to press the reset button and create a new blueprint for success. I could start the pursuit of my dream by sharing my journey.

I am the type of person that sees the glass as half full and the potential in everyone. I expect the power of God as I do my best to align myself with his will. We work to do the best we can and let God take care of the rest. Faith is a lifestyle choice for me. I have faced many challenges that would have otherwise stolen my joy, but by the grace of God I sustained a sense of peace. Obstacles, no matter how vast, do not have me or define me, but serve to refine me. I'm resolved to walk in full authority with an attitude of gratefulness that allows me to focus on blessings and not obstacles. You see, I have been blessed to have my mother, her mother, and her mother's mother modeled the same resolve and gratefulness. My mother is the reason I am who I am today. I came out of the womb blessed because of the women that came before me. I have a rich heritage of strong women whose underlying passion in life revolved around helping others. This Shift moment allowed me to realize this heritage does not have to stop with them.

This decision comes at a time when I am still trying to come to grips with my new role of widow and single mother. Why add another new thing to a plate that is already full? Am I willing to re-prioritize some things? What other things am I willing to give up? Am I willing to put in the work? Am I willing to play all-out? Am I committed? Am I willing to value myself?

My shift moment got me to my "Yes" moment. I am ready to pursue my passion and live in my purpose. I would like to share with you the first steps I took in getting to my "Next" to encourage you to take a first step of your own as you move into your o greatness one "next" at a time.

Understand Your Core Values

My core values serve as an anchor to keep me connected to my true self. Core values are deep beliefs fundamental to the decision-making processes. Decisions made with respect to the matters of life are tied deeply to core values. The evaluation of my core values brought clarity to why I was having some of the struggles in my life. I reviewed my list of values and ranked them to determine the top 10. I discovered one big thing was missing from the top five on my values list—my health. I then understood why five hours of sleep, missing workouts, and putting off doctor appointments was becoming a normal thing for me. My health was not the only discovery; I noticed that retirement was for many years ranked very high.

While understanding my core values, it became clear that subconsciously I was delaying my dreams until I retired, and that behavior was driven by the way I prioritized those values. My husband and I had talked about retirement; that he was going to play golf and relax, and I was going to finally be an author, speaker, and coach. The death of my husband was a reality check. He did not make it to retirement. So, I had to ask myself, "Can I afford to delay my dream any longer?" Your values may not change over the years but their ranking and priority will.

No gift or talent is too small when they are used by God to bless others. This is the exercise I used to understand my core values and write them down. I started with three simple questions, and then in my quiet time began to refine my list:

1. What things are you grateful for?
2. What things are important to you? List them and then go back and rank them.
3. What are your top ten core values?

Be honest with yourself. If you are struggling with a decision, revisit your core values. That will help you decide. These are your values and are not based on the opinions of others.

Write your Legacy Statement

"She inspired millions by living her life with purpose and integrity to help women and men stay focused through difficult times and to help them rise to the highest calling on their life. Her life helped others to remove the power from their trials and tribulations and step into and stay in their greatness."

Writing my legacy statement was another growth moment for me. I challenged myself to dream big. I found that I often dreamed at a level expected of me. Letting others drive my expectations so low that I was treating my dream like a hobby, instead of going all-out the way God planned. I challenged myself to dream in color, to embrace the possibilities and be prepared to walk boldly through the doors that God will open. It is my dream, and I will give it the value it deserves. Take the time to get to your why and write down your legacy statement. This statement may change as you grow but the foundation will remain the same and will be a cornerstone as you move into your next great thing. It is about how our lives can be used to help others.

Know what you bring to the table. The next step is a skills assessment. I had to take a step back and not look so much at the how, but look at the now. This exercise was a wakeup call for me because I learned I have natural gifts and talents that I did not place the right amount of value on. I did a personal skills inventory, and then informally polled those around me. Through this exercise I learned that I could bring my exceptional emotional intelligence, strategic thinking, business development, communications, coaching and management skills into play as I pursued my passion. Look at yourself inside and outside. Fully understand what you bring to the table and you will quickly find that you have talents and experience you can leverage during your journey. When I completed this process, I felt like God had been preparing me for this journey. Perspective is everything. Once you know what you are working with you can leverage that knowledge in working through your game plan. A lot of people underestimate what they bring to the table but God sees our potential. If we could only see ourselves the way He does. A dream is your creative vision for your life in the future. My challenge to you is to understand your value and your unique purpose. To leverage your shift moment like jet fuel that propels you to do and be more by embracing and elevating the gifts and talent you have been blessed with. No gift or talent is too small when they are used by God to bless others.

"You must break out of your current comfort zone and become comfortable with the unfamiliar and the unknown."
–Denis Waitley

Be willing to make yourself uncomfortable. Complacency is a weed that will eat away at your destiny if you are not careful. I was adjusting to my new normal and was blessed with a great support system. Things were finally predictable enough for me to start to relax. I had my routine down. I also found myself making one excuse after another for standing still. I had some good ones too. I am perfecting my craft, just one more class and I will have it down. I am doing my research. I will get started on Monday. I quickly learned that I had to work to make myself uncomfortable with the status quo. I had to integrate myself into a community of people that were a disruptive force and made me uncomfortable with standing still—not through judgment but through account-ability. I had to give the friends that loved me permission to hold me accountable. I actually called them up, stated the areas in which they could help me grow by holding me accountable and offered to do the same for them. Everyone has at least one of those friends that knows how to get the job done. It was time to stop talking about it and be about it. Time to step out in faith. That first step for me was to enter into the MTM Elite Coaching Certification program and engage myself into this new community.

Ask yourself—are you leveraging your gifts to enhance the lives of others, or are you still leaning on the excuses that are represented in well-worded milestones that must happen before you can begin? I challenge you to surround yourself with people that inspire you to grow, to do more and to be more. People that will partner with you to dream big while holding you accountable with respect to executing on your plan. Go to a conference or networking events that are attended by those doing what you want to do. People who are passionate about what they do, do not mind talking about it. You can't help but think bigger and stretch beyond your bound-aries when surrounded by amazing people doing amazing things.

Ask questions and understand their model of success. It is amazing who God will put in your path. Leverage every opportu-nity to grow. There were times I did not know a soul. I just smiled, introduced myself into the circle, and listened. I learned so much that way. These women elevated my thinking and showed me how to avoid a number of pitfalls. Be willing to seek out those who are like-minded and who are at the same place of growth that you are. You can compare notes. I have yet to leave a conference without expanding my circle.

Seek out best practices. Do your homework. Find a model of success that fits your personality. Find someone that is doing what you want to do and you like the way they are doing it. Work to understand what attracted you to them. Learn about their model of success. Invest in yourself. Yes it may mean giving up something. I had to cancel a girl's trip so I could attend training. I could have really used a beach in my life at that moment. I recommend getting a coach at some point. Do your homework and get the right coach. One of my biggest role models has four coaches. She leveraged them strategically to get her to the next level. Those coaches were experts in areas in which she wanted to grow in. We are quick to invest in training and coaching for our children in their activities; why is it so hard to value ourselves enough and do the same?

Create a blueprint. What is your game plan to move into the next phase of your life? Blueprint is basically a guide for making something based on what is known at the time. The good thing about a blueprint is it can be redrawn and expanded as you make new discoveries. There was freedom in knowing I did not have to have all the answers up front to begin my pursuit of my dreams. I could start where I was. I knew my core values, my strengths, and my desired impact. The blueprint represented a model that served as an anchor to my actions. When developing a blueprint you always start with a vision. For example, if you were to build your dream house, you would have a list of things, features, colors, and attributes that make it a dream home for you. What is your vision for your desired impact and next phase in your life? I started with a vision statement and transitioned that statement into a vision board. My blueprint was the foundational outline for my dream and my next step was to fill in the gaps and start the building process. Be excited about the possibilities your shift will bring. Remember one step at a time. The key is to keep moving—keep building.

My goals is to help others grow as I grow. My life was dramatically changed in three short months. Through it all, I learned a lot about the power of God and how to trust him. Even though I wondered why now and why my husband, it was a time of growth through many tears, fears, and heartache. In my heart I had to believe Charlie's death was not in vain. I have to wait for God to reveal His bigger plan. In faith I have resolved to not put my dreams on lay-a-way and to help others do the same.

My journey is just beginning. I would like to challenge you to join me, embrace your shift, and play all out. Here are some nuggets of wisdom I picked up along the way:

Protect your Vision: It is your vision; protect it. You may want to limit with whom you share your vision. God gave the vision to you not to them so everyone is not going to get it. Some may even discourage you. Do not place judgment; rather demonstrate the goodness of God as they see your dreams unfold. Let your life and pursuit of your dreams be the thing that helps them dream bigger.

Be Present and Take Time to Breathe: I have learned the importance of being present. How many blessing have we missed by not being in the moment? My son has taught me a lot about being present. He is so in tuned with nature that he is constantly pointing out the beauty of a sunset, the structure of the clouds in the sky, or the moon and stars at night. Unknowingly he invites me to stop the chatter in my head and appreciate the beauty in the things around me. He does this with a simple request to look up. I look up and in that moment I have many times found myself marveling at the power of God as I take in the beauty of what I am seeing. When you are present your head is no longer filled with past or future scenarios. You are just here, with your attention focused outward towards the person(s) you are interacting with or the place you are in. The removal of the mind chatter allows you to take time to breathe and take it all in. How many beautiful things have you missed because you did not slow down enough to be present? These beautiful things are not limited to nature. A beautiful thing can be nugget of wisdom because you were present in a conversation. An innovative thought that came from you having quiet time in which you are taking time to be present with yourself. I challenge you to take time to breathe and be present.

Attitude of Gratitude: I challenge you to start each day with thoughts of gratitude. List at least five things without even trying, and grow the list daily. I love catching God taking care of me. Pay attention and you will see the same.

Walk your walk: Comparison is the thief of joy and derails dreams. Learning from other is one thing but comparing yourself to others is another. Trust God to order your steps.

Play all-out—Do your best: Do not underplay your hand because others are uncomfortable with the speed of your success. Your real friends will be happy for you.

Fail Forward: The goal is not to avoid failures along the way. The goal is leveraging those failures to make you stronger and use them as opportunities for growth.

Expect big things: I challenge you to dream big while focusing on the journey step by step. When you reach one milestone, do not be afraid to add another one and reach higher.

BE PRESENT IN THE MOMENT— MOMENTS PERISH

CHERYL LUMPKIN

"If you surrender completely to the moments as they pass, you live more richly those moments."

–Anne Morrow Lindbergh

Opening my eyes after surgery to debilitating pain threw me into a tailspin. I realized right away I was not longer in control but at the mercy of everyone around me. The burden immediately was how would I learn to ask for help. The gentle touch of my daughter placing my stud in my nose assured me that everything was going to be all right. That familiar feeling of her warm hands reassured me that I had been spared and granted another opportunity to fulfill my life's purpose, to pursue the dreams and desires of my heart. While drifting back to sleep, all I could focus on was the pain and the items on my "To Do" list. I just wanted relief, but I started to understand that I had to be present in the moment. I no longer could sit on the sidelines cheering someone on, I had to be an active participant in the healing process. Regaining my strength, appreciating good health was going to be a collective effort of attitude, fortitude, and determination. What I discovered is that I needed assistance from many sources to guide me through this process. Foregoing pride, ego, and my way, I had to trust that the teachers of the universe would shift my perspective and allow me to grow in many ways.

In those first few hours, all I could focus on was how I was going to manage through this process and have full recovery and mobility of my knee. Because of that, I forgot to give gratitude for being given an opportunity to see another day. I was charged with moving and standing by my Physical Therapist who was extremely supportive and knowledgeable of the process of putting me on the healing path. As we discussed my rehabilitation goals, I realized that I would have to trust his methods and relinquish control. Quickly I decided that he knew what was best for my care; however, I had a checklist of items I wanted to accomplish to put me back in the driver's seat.

I'd been hoping for the past few years that I could avoid the inevitable fact that I would have to undergo surgery on my knee. I witnessed my mom and brother undergo the same procedure and thought for some unknown reason it would bypass me. For several years, I tried all the options, which included physical therapy, water aerobics, Chinese and modern medicine to minimize the pain and increase mobility, until I finally gathered the courage to proceed with the knee replacement. I tended to gravitate to articles about the procedure and recovery process which had favorable outcomes. I refused to read much about possible complications because I figured it didn't apply to me. The lesson I learned is that you have to take a balanced approach when facing critical decisions. I put my blinders on in an effort to skip through the process without being present in the moment.

On day two after my surgery, I lay in bed imagining how I got here. For most of my life I pretended to be a Super Woman because up until now, I had never needed help. I had been a caretaker to my mother who succumbed to cancer and my elderly grandmother. And now I found myself stressing over asking for help to go to the bathroom. That thought took me away from thinking long term and put me right in the moment.

Just the sheer joy of taking a shower alone in the hospital was something I never could have foreseen if I hadn't been in this place I found myself. The freedom I felt was unbelievable. At home my shower was my prayer closet, the place I released everything to God and watched my problems, anxieties, and fears go down the drain. I took those moments for granted, and once I was getting a taste of it in the hospital I could have stayed there forever.

Up until my illness, my focus was traveling to Cuba, completing my next writing projects, developing a comprehensive social media strategy for my business, crawling on the floor with children, and much more. My list of things to do was endless and provided me an opportunity to minimize and escape from the journey facing me. What I didn't anticipate was that there would be bumps in the road that would serve as distractors from the path I was on. I wasn't prepared for digging deeper, pushing harder, and yes sometimes screaming louder than I ever have to climb this mountain. Having to pull out all the stops, I'm gleaning lessons in faith, gratitude, humility, trust, and patience and how important these qualities are to my recovery. Although challenging, I'm using them to get me where I need to be.

Faith

"Faith allows things to happen. It is the power that comes from a fearless heart. And when a fearless heart believes, miracles happen."

–Author unknown

On day two after surgery, my Physical Therapist asked me what my personal goals were and we decided to make a plan. Being very ambitious and determined to be on the road to recovery I had one major goal. My focus was on regaining my independence and climbing 18 steps to my house. Of course I didn't have a backup plan because I never took into consideration that the healing process would be more difficult than expected. On day three, we decided to venture to the staircase in the hospital for me to attempt to achieve my goal. As we maneuvered down the halls, I started to realize that it was exhausting and that maybe I was being a bit ambitious. The closer we got to the door of the staircase I realized that fear of not completing the goal faced me. The beauty of my therapist is that he took me to the edge and allowed me to determine that I was not prepared for this step in the recovery progress. I took one step and fear started to creep into my mind. All I could imagine in my mind was that I was going to fall to the bottom of the staircase and create more problems. As discouraged as I was at not being able to complete this task, he assured me that I would be able to master it in a few days if I had patience and determination. He stated, "Take one step at a time. Stop worrying about the end result." The gift of wisdom he had at the moment, helped to lift my spirit and made me surrender control. I realized that a shift in character was in order and I needed to have faith in miracles. There was a time and place for everything and it was critical for my recovery that I celebrate each milestone by being present in the moment.

When I felt steady and in control, I tended to rely on my own strength, or so I thought. But as I struggled for control and allowed fear to creep in, I realized how important faith was for getting me from one step to the other. I began to worry less about long-term goals and more of the immediate challenges that were before me.

Humility

"Humility is the only true wisdom by which we prepare our minds for all the possible changes of life."
–George Arliss

The journey to recovery was filled with many lessons. As I adjusted to rehabilitation, I found myself becoming extremely restless and anxious wanting to accelerate the healing process. I had an aging roommate who would whimper in pain as the nursing staff cared for her. The impatience I felt made me get up on the walker. I was fearful that my aging roommate would impact my attitude and decided to stroll down the hall to the nurse's station for a breath of fresh air. I was so worried about becoming that woman that I tried to hide from the reality that I was just as needy. While talking with the nurses, a man in a wheelchair decided to come join our conversation. As he shared his health challenges, I realized that he was an amputee who had the courage to deliver an important message to me on humility. He stated that with all his problems he was going to fight for his independence and stop complaining about what he couldn't do at that moment. He encouraged me to be present in the moment, allow people to help me in my journey, and to pay attention to others who were in need. His words of wisdom made me walk the hall of shame as I returned to my room. Instead of feeling sorry for myself, I decided to embrace my fear of being that person yelling out in pain, and surrender to being humble and grateful for small accomplishments.

When I returned to my room, my aging roommate was crying to the nurse. She was saying that she felt all alone and wanted her daughter to be there. The nurse had the most angelic voice and said, "You are not alone. I will sit with you all day until your daughter arrives." Her patience and kind words brought tears to my eyes, as I knew that message was meant for me as well. While her gentle words were meant for my roommate, I started to pay attention to my journey and understand the importance of being present in the moment instead of thinking ahead about where I should be in my recovery process.

A shift in perspective started to occur as I realized that sometimes I had to go to my lowest point so I could rise like the phoenix sun. My lesson in humility was fraught with the kindness of angels who were surrounding and teaching me with nuggets of gold that would strengthen my character. I decided to buckle up, stop complaining, and embrace the rough road ahead. What I discovered is that regardless of my situation, the universe would give me insight and allow me to become stronger in my walk. I never would have known the power of humility had I not faced certain challenges. I found that humility is multi-dimensional and that with a greater self-understanding and awareness, I could be open with my thoughts, words, and deeds.

Gratitude

"At times, our own light goes out and is rekindled by a spark from another person. Each of us has cause to think with deep gratitude of those who have lighted the flame within us."
–Albert Schweitzer

Going through the recovery process requires an extreme shift of mental, physical, and emotional healing. I put gratitude on the sideline without thoroughly examining its true value. Don't get me wrong, I didn't dismiss gratitude, I just minimized how impactful it would be to my recovery. Yes I was grateful that I was awakened from surgery and the doctor stated that it went well. But I could not focus on this gift because I was so consumed with the pain in my knee. I could not understand why most people said it was the best decision they made and that even though the rehabilitation was grueling I would be able to bounce back like new. It's important to do our due diligence, read the fine print, and weigh possible outcomes that can shape and shift your perspective.

A few days later while in PT with about 35 people, I heard a patient scream out in excruciating pain. The scream was so piercing that everyone stopped to see what was happening. The room immediately became silent and many patients put their heads downs because they could identify with the lady who had the courage to release it to the world. Suddenly many patients started to gravitate to the woman to show her encouragement. We created a circle around her as she worked with her Physical Therapist and applauded her accomplishments. As tears rolled down our faces, I saw in her heart and spirit a sense of gratitude as she continued to be sparked by the fire of encouragement.

I have found that in many situations I forget to give gratitude for simple accomplishments. Being so consumed with immediate results, I find myself sidetracked and resentful that my goals are not happening fast enough. What I have come to accept is that being grateful allows me to open my heart and mind to new and different perspectives. I no longer focus on being a victim in a situation where I have no control. Instead of asking, "Why am I the one who has to have complications with this procedure?" I have shifted my perspective and ask myself, "What can I learn from this experience, and how do I help others understand the importance of gratitude?"

I have reached out to my nieces and nephews and asked them to explain to me what gratitude means to them. They have stated to never give up on the dreams and desires of your heart and to always be thankful. They reminded me that they wouldn't be where they are today had it not been for their ancestors and friends who have paved the way. One of my nieces said to be grateful for the small steps and accomplishments, because many people in my situation can't stand. I realize the importance of being grateful for the little things which helped me to appreciate and accept the small milestones.

Patience

"Patience is not passive; on the contrary, it is active; it is concentrated strength."
–Edward G. Bulwer-Lytton

Patience has never been my strong suit so I decided to test my relationship to it and provide it a much needed tune-up. While putting down my armor, defenses, and setting my ego aside, I became more vulnerable and open to new perspectives. Instead of focusing on why all of these life lessons were surrounding me, I made the conscious effort to submit willingly to the universe and embrace its complexity.

My whole focus of patience was tied to being able to climb 18 steps to my house. What I had to learn was that each step was a move forward and that I couldn't rush to the end without appreciating each milestone and the view from different perspectives. I learned that if my focus was so much on tomorrow and what it would bring, then I wouldn't be present in this specific moment and time. I would have missed an opportunity to rest and reflect on my accomplishments. Regardless of how small they might have seemed, I needed to acknowledge its value.

The beauty of quiet time is that you have a chance to step outside of yourself and forge a oneness with the universe. You have time to examine your core views and determine which ones require adjustments. As I reflected on the nurse saying to the patient, "You are not alone...," I started to ponder and seek understanding of those powerful words. In that moment, to connect with her patient, the nurse needed to be very active in offering strength and support while exhibiting patience.

When we practice patience, we discover an energy, which can affect us in a positive or negative manner. There were many days in physical therapy where I was discouraged and impatient with my progress. The machines were difficult to operate and I couldn't see any progress. My spirit became broken and I couldn't visualize nor understand why this was happening to me. It was during these critical moments that my physical therapist extended his hand and words of encouragement.

Trust

> "*Trust is a core currency of any relationship. Sometimes our need to control and micromanage everything erodes our confidence in ourselves and others. The truth: People are much more capable than we think. A hearty dose of trust is often what's needed to unlock the magic. Go ahead, have faith.*"
>
> –Kris Carr

Never undervalue the power of trust and how it impacts your mental state of being. I have come to realize that there is a secret power in trusting that things will work out. Many times I found myself doubting and questioning why situations were happening and why they are contrary to my plan. Trust has become a key element in this recovery journey. It's never easy to relinquish control and depend on others for assistance. My personal values and lessons are linked directly to my ability to display a need for control. Many times throughout this process, I have had to surrender control and allow myself to trust people around me to support me through these unsteady times.

Trust is a fundamental emotion, which builds character based on mutual respect and integrity. I never knew that trust would be such an integrated part of the healing process. When faced with challenges, I have always thought that I would figure it out by myself. What I have discovered is that in order to trust you have to rely on others to provide you strength and courage.

I have been fortunate to have teachers of trust in this recovery process. The beauty of my teachers in this stage is that they realized that I needed help and that because of ego and stubbornness I had to show a willingness to accept my current situation and be vulnerable in that moment. I needed to confront my fear of falling and allow them to guide me to safety. I experienced many critical lessons in trust and I'm starting to understand the power it has in character building.

One of my friends attempted to help me off the curb as I was attempting to maneuver with my cane. Struggling for independence and wanting to show off my progress I resisted her assistance and almost fell. As I struggled in that moment to regain balance, I had to allow myself to surrender and to be thankful that she was by my side to support my next move. I realized the importance of gratitude and needed to share with her my shortcomings in the area of trust and ask for forgiveness for being ungrateful for the assistance. Sometimes we find ourselves being so stubborn and resistant that it impedes our progress.

One day while working out on the equipment, I struggled to get off the machine. My physical therapist extended her hand in an effort to offer me assistance to stand. I paused for a moment as I decided to allow myself to surrender control and defer to her wise counsel. What I appreciated is that when she saw me withdraw and ponder my next move, she kept her hand extended until I trusted her enough to allow her to guide me with my next move. In many situations be it personal or professional, guides will appear to empower us to dig deep into our souls and modify our responses. This was a powerful moment in that I realized that I was not alone on this journey and that she was going to hold me accountable for shifting my perspective.

In order for me to fully recover, I would have to trust and seek greater understanding of the role I played in not only physical but also mental rehabilitation. The beauty of learning to trust is that I had to dispel the superwoman myth.

Many times we find ourselves so consumed with the next project, future goals, or next steps that we question our understanding or appreciate our current state of being. We tend to put gratitude, faith, and humility on the shelf while we navigate our journey. In those critical moments we start to spiral downwards, when there seems to be no end in sight, when we rely on our ways and think we are in control. We want everything to be happy immediately and fail to understand that sometimes the greatness comes in character building.

The beauty of this entire process is that I have been enlightened and encouraged to push forward even when it seems impossible. What I realize is that physical rehabilitation works in conjunction with mental courage and it's not for the faint of heart. You must have courage to admit when you are spiraling out of control and feeling depressed. What's critical to understand is that so often we are afraid to ask for help because of our pride and ego. It is during those low and lonely moments that we have to reach out to someone to help navigate through this phase. We have to realize that we are not alone in our struggles and that family, friends, and angels are sent to us to teach us valuable life lessons. The key is that I have had to become receptive to finding new solutions to the challenges and work closely with my sports physical therapists to strengthen my knee.

I challenge you to confront your fears, and start shedding excessive baggage that holds you back from being the best you can be. Shift your attitudes, beliefs, and began to heal your mind, body, and spirit. I discovered that by relinquishing control, I was actually aligning myself with my universal plan. True power and control exist only when you let go and allow yourself to be present in the moment. I no longer take good health and recovery as a given, nor ask the question, "Why me?" Instead, I allow myself to dig deeper for understanding and remember that faith, humility, gratitude, patience, and trust will help me to walk taller and lean on others when the road seems rough. I am truly grateful for all my teachers in this rehabilitation process who have taught me these lessons and supported me as I gain courage to try harder. I no longer look to paying it back, but I will be more mindful and deliberate as I pay it forward.

"To enjoy good health, to bring true happiness to one's family, to bring peace to all, one must first discipline and control one's own mind. If a man can control his mind, he can find the way to Enlightenment, and all wisdom and virtue will naturally come to him."

–Buddha

LOVE WILL...

BY SCOTT COZART

"The greatest measuring stick for love is the degree to which one will sacrifice in order to express it."

–Scott Cozart

A middle-aged man whom I had never met appeared at my front door and handed me a regular sized white envelope with a few sheets of folded paper inside. Divorce papers. It was so strange; I didn't even have to sign for it. It was May 2013 and I was on the phone with a very close friend at the time, and he instructed me to put it away and not read it; I had heavier responsibilities requiring my attention.

I continued packing to vacate the home I shared with my wife and children. While cleaning the garage I saw a black trash bag on the floor. Immediately I heard the Lord say to my spirit, "Make sure you're not throwing away anything important in there." I placed my hand in the bag only to pull out used cups, discarded papers, crumpled fast-food bags, and other trash. As I reached the bottom of the bag I felt what seemed to be a heavy book. I grabbed it firmly and pulled it out. It had a beautiful oceanic blue cover with a multitude of white clouds draped across the front and back. It had my wife's name and the word "journal" written on the outside cover. Momentarily I felt as if I was Harrison Ford acting out a great archaeological discovery scene in the "Raiders of the Lost Ark" movie. Though I wanted to read it, I didn't and followed suit with the advice I had received moments ago concerning the divorce papers. I put my bible, the papers, and the journal away in my storage unit.

It was August 2002 when I answered a phone call from my soon to be wife. I briefly met her during a campus event in Knoxville, Tennessee where she was a campus minister and keyboardist for an international college organization. We talked about the ministry and fundraising for this Christian organization on campus. Our cordial exchange was pleasant and made me smile. Those few minutes turned into months of conversations, and I'd soon be in love. I felt in my spirit she would be my wife, so February 2003 I drove to Tennessee from North Carolina to meet with her. She was lovely. Her smile framed a room, her skin was a deep rich brown, and she had a slender but shapely athletic build. Yes, I was in love! I washed her feet in a basin of water, dried them with a soft white towel, carefully massaged them with a special perfumed light olive oil, and asked her to marry me. Of course she said yes. I think the pleasure in her feet caused her mind to drift and left her mouth open to say anything at that point.

We were married on May 31, 2003 in Chattanooga, Tennessee. I was the happiest man alive. That day was bright and beautiful, and I was certain that throughout the years we would watch our hair change from as black as pepper to as white as salt. Instead of our hair changing colors, it was the wedding that seemed to quickly shift from a deep red to a cloudy and stormy gray. I was so excited to enter our luxury hotel room after racing from the limousine. However, my excitement soon turned to deep disappointment. Instead of expressing our love, she suggested we sleep. I could feel the mood getting worse and worse. When she finally awoke she asked me not to kiss on her or caress her, saying she wasn't interested in any pre-consummating activities. She just laid there silently with her eyes peeled off to the corner of the dimly lit room. Her body language, her eyes, and her words all quietly shouted to me that she did not want to be there, and I felt confused and deeply conflicted.

When our first-time intimate experience was over she scurried out of bed and rushed to the bathroom. There was no kiss, no hug, or even a tender exchange of, "I love you." I laid in the bed as tears tip-toed down my face. I couldn't understand why this experience was different from the one I had so vividly imagined and hoped for. She stayed in the bathroom so long that I eventually fell asleep and was only awakened by the noise of the bathroom door. I asked her if she was okay and she replied by saying yes and goodnight. Instead of turning it into a painful argument I chose to remain quiet and hoped she would change. She never did. Our life together wasn't perfect. As I reflected, we really didn't spend much time together to form a bond with each other before marriage. There was no court-ship and I soon realized she wasn't an affectionate person.

On the outside things appeared pretty normal. My wife didn't work, choosing rather to start a family and stay at home, to which I agreed. Within four months of marriage, I was begging for intimacy from her, and then she hit me right between the eyes when she said, "I really don't like sex," and she really didn't like to be touched.

Within five years we had three small children and had moved from Kentucky to Tennessee. She was a fulltime student at a prestigious theological seminary, and I worked nights while keep-ing the children during the day. Though I was not present on campus often, the students, professors, and faculty really liked me. Within a couple of years, even though she was more visible and more involved in the community, the students and faculty began referring to her as "Scott's wife," which I believe she grew to resent. A year later I became an employee of the seminary and we became closely connected with an internationally famous reli-gious personality. My wife was simply enthralled. This person adopted my family as her own and we really became a close-knit unit. We had a fourth child on the way when I was invited by this person to preach at a large event alongside high profile preachers. It would have made me happy if she had been able to come, but she was pregnant and could not travel. While the opportunity was an open door for me, I could tell she wouldn't have minded if it slammed in my face. She appeared jealous because I had been chosen over her. She loved being in the limelight, and wanted the fame and fortune that came with it. I didn't understand why this opportunity made her even more distant from me; as if more distance was possible.

When we moved to Georgia, I began my graduate degree program in Atlanta, and my wife gave birth to a fifth child. Although we had five children, it was rare that we were together intimately because often she made herself unavailable. It was like going to Chick-fil-A on Sunday. No matter how much I wanted it, I just couldn't get it. And then our marriage got dramatically worse.

On Saturday morning, April 27th I walked into the kitchen around 9 A.M. and asked if anyone wanted breakfast. Her sharp reply was, "Everybody in this house has been up since 7 A.M.!" Her tone had always been sharp but that morning she seemed more determined to argue. Shortly after shouting at me, she called her mom and left to stay overnight. She returned home early Monday morning and slept on the couch. When we drove the kids to school there were often long pauses of silence as I attempted to understand what was going on with my wife. Once back home, I sat at the dining room table as she stood folding clothes while continuing the discussion. She eventually left to pick the children up from school and never returned home. Frantically I called, left voice mails, and texted her, but she didn't respond to any of them. I realized three things that day: she folded their clothes right in front of my face, she left me without even saying why or goodbye, and she had taken away the heartbeat of my soul—my precious innocent children. And worst of all, she was three months pregnant with our sixth child.

Unable to bear the rejection, and being unable to see my children, I suffered a heart attack while driving from the gym four days later. The pain was so intense I literally had to drive to the hospital with my knees. The staff rushed me in and ran tests until late that evening. There was a 99 percent blockage in my artery and they performed surgery early the next morning.

Life moved forward and much of what happened became sort of a blur; my life for several months was a blur. I remember being in pain physically as I walked across the stage to receive my master's degree, and driving to North Carolina to visit my mother. She had been diagnosed with breast cancer and her health was rapidly declining. My siblings and I gathered around her bedside and prayerfully watched her transition into eternal life. It was uniquely the most beautiful and yet hardest thing I've ever experienced. Though I released her hands, I held her ever so tightly in my heart.

It was only fifteen days after my surgery and now my mom had passed away. When I called my wife to inform her my mom had passed away, her casual and uninterested reply was, "Huh… really?" It was devoid of any care, concern, or empathy. She didn't ask how I was doing or about my family. In fact, she would not even let my children attend the funeral. Two days later, my brother and I eulogized my mother's funeral. Preaching through the pain of her death, and the loss of my family was agonizing. And still, no one knew my wife had left and took my children. In fact, I couldn't even tell my dad until a couple of weeks after the funeral, because he needed time to grieve for his wife of more than 50 years.

The same day I buried my mom, I would have celebrated my tenth year wedding anniversary. I silently grieved the passing of my mom and secretly bemoaned the loss of my marriage and the forced distance between my children and me. My father, siblings, and a few close friends were so supportive. Whatever I needed they were only a phone call away. Often they would just send money or a word of encouragement without being prompted. About a week later, I returned to Georgia, went to my storage unit, and retrieved my bible with the envelope that held the divorce papers and the journal underneath it.

I drove to the public library, sat in an empty room, and read the divorce decree. I was paralyzed with confusion as I read false allegations of mental abuse, physical abuse, and adultery. I couldn't figure out why someone would make up the most deplorable lies just to leave a marriage. Leaving the marriage didn't require lying, it only required leaving. My wife wanted everything including money, furniture, full custody of the kids, vehicles, and even garden tools among many other requests. As I continued to read, one part struck me as odd. She demanded everything except child support for the sixth but unborn child. Why would a woman who wants everything not want anything for the sixth child?

I then picked up her journal and read years of her accumulated dirty secrets. I didn't realize the level of planning that had been happening around me for a long time. I sat in shock and cried all over again, because I realized there was a great possibility that the unborn baby may not be my biological child.

My wife was in a relationship with a married man, who was also affiliated with the ministry she served, and was possibly pregnant with his child. After reading her journal it was obvious that she never really loved me and quite clear that she was in love with someone else. How sad and deceived I was. The facts made me feel so small and foolish. My mind skimmed back over the years of her coming home at 3 A.M. and late night phone calls in the driveway as I watched from the window. Remembering her claims of studying in her professor's office and falling asleep in the driveway were all an attempt to cover up her affair. My heart sank with a heavy helplessness and rejection as I thought back through the marriage that was obviously over.

It was here that I shifted! I am the most gentle, compassionate, patient, and understanding man I know. I imagined she and her mom thought I would leave Georgia, return to North Carolina a weak and broken man in poor health, forget all about my children, and remain out of their sight and thus out of their minds. However, they were wrong. I decided I would fight back with a righteous responsibility and a moral obligation. My weapons would be chosen from the closet of prayer and not the basement of revenge.

Over my life, I spent a lot of time in the basement. Not the basement of revenge, just the basement of being lost in the darkness of life. There was a time I focused only on women, drinking, and partying. After observing my parents' relationship, I made a promise to the Lord to be the best husband possible and never be unfaithful to my wife.

When I first went away to college, as a much younger man, my moral compass did not always point north. The ratio of young ladies to guys was 20:1. It was simply unbelievable; my life felt like a dream. At the second college I attended, my first intimate contact was with a university librarian. I skipped right over the girls at the university and began my activities with the administrative staff, because I thought it would increase my market value on campus, and it did. In fact, it was so bad that I was told that if I were caught again in the girl's dorm on campus without being properly signed in they would expel me from school. I was selfish, had too many choices, and cared very little about anyone else's interest in a relationship other than my own. Emotionally I hurt a lot of people unnecessarily and it makes me sad to think about that.

On October 1, my senior year in college, I changed my life and followed the Lord. From that day forward I was on a mission to be the best person and future husband I could possibly be. I was deeply determined to treat everyone with a high degree of dignity and respect. Though my wife hated me, and yes it did hurt, but not enough to change my resilient approach to unconditional love. *Nobody* can force me down so low, as to hate everyone else and no one can propel me so high as to love only myself. I love because there lives in me no other alternative.

I immediately sprang into action and found a high profile attorney in my city. We met on Friday morning at his office. He required five thousand dollars in sum and a three thousand dollar retaining fee, which had to be paid to him in cash by Monday morning as he was leaving for vacation Monday afternoon.

Saturday morning I sat in a Walgreen's parking lot praying to the Lord and asking what I should do. I had nothing. The Lord instructed me to call my dad in North Carolina and assemble a group of men, 70 or older, who were pillars in my community from my hometown. I called him and within an hour the meeting was set for 6 P.M. that evening. When I drove there from Atlanta I was broken and worn. The men sat quietly and listened with stunned but supportive looks on their faces. Among the men present was my mentor and long time family friend, my dad's kind brother, his generous cousin, and his faithful boyhood friend. As I finished speaking they all gave money and one of them wrote me a check for six thousand and five hundred dollars. I wept with humility. I felt supported by a defensed wall of seasoned men.

I returned to Georgia and paid the attorney. After three short face-to-face meetings within two months, I had given him all the money I had and yet very little had been done for my case. I wrote him a 22-page letter concerning things I didn't understand. For instance, why we were not going to trial when I had specifically requested a trial to prove my innocence. I had even asked my family to come. The trial was granted but when the money ran out, he asked the Judge to be removed from my case. The only good thing he had done was follow through on my refusal to accept anything less than joint legal and joint physical custody of my children. Ultimately, I went to court for two years without an attorney present.

Even though it seemed like everyone had left me except my faithful family and a few close friends, the Lord was always present with me. I secured employment at a local elementary school teaching the game of chess to students from kindergarten through fifth grade. I sought this schedule because I started work at 2:30 P.M., which allowed me to visit with my children at their school during lunch. This made me happy and sad. Happy because I got to see them, but sad because they would cry terribly when I left. Taking my children from me was the cruelest and most painful thing anybody has ever done to me.

Throughout my wife's pregnancies, I went to every appointment, every ultrasound, and every doctor's visit. I witnessed the birth of each child. I cut their umbilical cords and even gave my fifth child his first bath right after birth. Whether playing in the park, or jumping into a pile of freshly raked leaves, I was there playing with them and enjoying every minute of it.

I knew I would have to give an account to the Lord for my actions during the divorce and one day my children would ask concerning my behavior. I needed to be able to tell them the truth and demonstrate for them that winning was not necessarily better than pleasing. In so many ways they saw me experience physical losses but they saw me please the Lord by treating their mother well and doing the right thing. I had to set an example showing them how to be and remain pleasing even when things were not pleasant. I didn't have to lie on her to get my way. I knew that if I showed her mercy the Lord would record it, remember it, and reward me for it. Letting go of anything or anybody that you love is always difficult especially when it's not your choice. When she left me I still loved her.

I pushed to get myself together emotionally and financially. I had to train myself to love my wife differently, not less. I will not decrease my capacity to love or the energy by which I love, just because I was hurt. Later I worked as a parking lot attendant at a local high school for just over minimum wage. Within a few weeks my principal offered me a position as the assistant men's basketball coach for the freshman, junior varsity, and varsity teams, and eventually a teaching position in the areas of biology, earth science, and physical science. Though the money was important, being on the exact same schedule as my children was the ultimate goal.

Two years after our divorce battle, my wife and her attorney eventually had to sign the divorce decree that I had written myself. It encompassed all things that were in the best interest of the children and my ability to spend time with them. After three DNA tests, the precious little girl born two years earlier was happily proven to be my daughter. My six children, four boys and two girls, love me deeply and long for the day they can live with me. As for love, my eyes are opened; my heart is still soft, my arms still stretched wide for a new love, and my mind is focused on rebuilding. Upon opening my eyes to a beautiful and new love, I imagine with a smile that some Godly and charming woman will be looking for a man just like me.

Along my journey, I've learned:

There are times in life where it is important to lose or suffer temporary loss, for the purpose of a fuller, sustainable life. The Lord showed me how to win big at losing and taught me how to lose well.

When you provide the pen of hope and love, patience will write your story.

A man that controls his own spirit is mightier than a man that takes a whole city.

The reason I remained in my marriage was because I vowed to the Lord that I would stay for better or worse and I truly hoped things would get better throughout the years. In reflection, I would have had an actual courtship before the marriage. Learning your partner and their tendencies is crucial as it helps to reveal and define compatibility. Do not rush or be rushed into anything! I did not investigate my spouse. It is wise to discuss past relationships, finances, and family. There is a time for private and fragile things to be shared, but whenever asked all things must be answered honestly. If you fail to answer honestly from the beginning, you will appear to have purposely manipulated the truth and thus break trust between you and your partner.

As a father I learned that I am still their leader and head of their house, even though I do not physically live with them. Removing a father from the house and separating him from his children does not take away his position or the authority he has. It is a God-given position. It is a position that was created in eternity. I realized no one could remove me from my post of prayer and leadership fueled by an all-enduring love.

When attempting to choose a spouse in the traditional sense there are a few things that should be considered.

- As a man, choose someone who will provide a safe and respected place for you to be heard.
- As a woman, choose someone who will relate to you based on the truth that the Lord has said about you.
- Both parties should choose someone who is able to suffer well with them.
- Let no one control or bait you into regrettable fits of anger and revenge.

Suffering is love accompanied by tears and love is suffering expressed through a smile. Constantly think on what's true and ask yourself the questions that matter. Are love and suffering fraternal twins or first cousins? Are winning and losing archenemies or competitive friends? Are pain and joy complete strangers or siblings separated at birth? Keep seeking truth and never give up when things get difficult. I challenge you to buy land and build your house on the high road. That's a moral choice you can make and invest in. Begin your morning's there. The high road is not some fancy detoured trail you occasionally struggle to hike when things don't go your way. It's where you should eat, rest, and conclude your evenings. Keep clean hands while traveling the dusty and dirty roads of life. Love as if no other alternative lives in you. Love is generally found just beyond the sign that reads, "The Extra Mile."

"The greatest measuring stick for love is the degree to which one will sacrifice in order to express it."

–Scott Cozart

LEARNING TO BE STILL

CHERYL POLOTE-WILLIAMSON

"Be still and know that I am God."

Psalm 46:10

"You don't know that God is all you need until God is all you have."

–Rick Warren

This quote rings in my head like clanging symbols with a lasting note that reverberates every time I repeat it to myself. In fact if you say these words to yourself they will deliver you from places only God could have brought you from.

New Jersey was that place for me. After moving four previous times to support my husband's career, this Southern Belle was headed *back* to New Jersey. I spent over a year crying, pleading, and making deals with God. I said, "Lord, if You make a way for me to stay in Texas, I'll go to church every Sunday. I'll be nicer to people I really don't care for, and I'll take time to pray 3 to 4 hours a day."

I wasn't ready for another change. I was happy with my life just the way it was. We had been living in Texas for seven years and I was at the top of my game with a successful career, our children were excelling in school, and we had a wonderful church and great friends. Needless to say after all my bargaining with God, I didn't keep my end of the bargain. I still went to church, but not as often as I should, and I didn't make an extra effort to be kind to others. I'm laughing now because who did I think I was to bargain with God?

Much to my chagrin, I was the one who had to sell our home, pack up the children, purchase a new home, and move to New Jersey all before the end of the school year. I was mad at God and a few other people as well. When I say I was mad, I'm talking being super ticked off at everybody, but especially God. Why did I have to pack up my family again? Why did we have to move to cold, expensive, not-so-friendly (in my opinion at the time) New Jersey? When we exited the plane in New Jersey it was cold and rainy. I said to myself, "Come on now, it's April and we're in coats for Easter."

At this point God and I were still not on good terms. I couldn't believe He was making me leave a place I loved to bring me back to the very place I told him I would never return. That's right, I had told God eight years prior that I would "never" return to New Jersey. Well, I guess He showed me who was really in control.

The ride from the airport was the longest ride of my life. My face got tighter and tighter and not so pleasant words were running all through my head. As we passed through certain towns to get to our home I could see my children in the back seat becoming very uneasy. I was growing angrier and less spiritual by the minute. When we reached the front door of our new home the kids breathed a sigh of relief; the house *was* beautiful. As I walked up to the door and turned the key I said, "God, Whatever you want me to learn in this place teach me quickly because I can't stay indefinitely." I sat on the top of my luggage weeping so hard that I felt I would vomit. I remember thinking there's got to be more to life than chasing after the next promotion and starting over again every few years.

The more I thought about it, the more I fell into despair. I felt lost, frustrated, angry, and just downright hurt. My husband left early for work every day, and I would get the kids off to schools they didn't like in weather conditions they were not accustomed to. I was lonely and disappointed. Let's just say momma was not happy therefore the house was not happy.

I felt disenfranchised so I was in no rush to find a new church home and when I finally did, let's just say we could have stood up every Sunday when they asked if there were any visitors. Although the members of the church were kind and engaging, I wasn't where I needed to be mentally or spiritually. I know now God took me to that place to get my attention; however, I was not the least bit interested in church or Bible study on a consistent basis like I had been before. My mindset was to just go to church, pay my tithes, and get home. In my mind, praying and begging and pleading with God didn't do any good so, what would be different this time around?

Well, just as I had requested, God showed me what He wanted me to learn. He taught me: *"Do everything possible on your part to live in peace with everyone" (Romans 12:18).* My first lesson came through a very serious bullying incident that could have cost my son his life. It happened within the first few months of the new school year. My son is 6'1" with green eyes and a fair complexion; an honor student who speaks the King's English. This was a recipe for disaster in this new culture. His school in Texas was mostly upper middle class suburban predominantly white students, but now he was in a very diverse school that included some lower middle class urban students who had no interest in learning.

Surviving in this new environment required a great deal of self-confidence, which my son seemed to be lacking. The multiple moves and new schools had taken a toll on his confidence, self-esteem, and self-worth. My son felt he didn't fit the mold so he decided to "dumb down" by lowering his academic standard and was released from his honors classes. I did everything I could to get him back in. Notice I said, **"I"** which is a sure sign of pride and arrogance.

My son started hanging with the 'homeboys' who didn't care about going to class; they were too busy causing problems. One kid in particular decided to make my son's life miserable by tormenting him every day. For months I was a nervous wreck while my son was at school. I wouldn't even let him walk home. It was time for a conversation with God. I asked, "You moved me here for this? What's the lesson?" My son is unhappy, scared, and does not want to attend school.

On one fateful day when I picked up my son from school, I saw him walking down the sidewalk at a fast pace. A group of boys were pushing him from behind. I began to sweat and my heart was racing. I knew I had to do *something*. As my son approached the car I noticed he was sweating and his clothes were dirty. I asked him what happened. The boys were getting closer.

He said, "They jumped me and hit me in the back of the head."

All of a sudden anger, rage, and a fire boiled inside me that I could not control. I remember praying, "God please protect me in this." I jumped out of my truck and told my son to get inside and wait with my girls. My girls were crying and asking me to get back into the car, saying, "Mommy, don't do this!" But by then my adrenaline was pumping and I psyched myself up. I think it was my prayer for God's protection that spared me that day.

Before I knew it I was on the curb; all 5 feet, 7½ inches and 145 pounds was surrounded by six boys. It was a total out of body experience. I remember asking them what the problem was, and they responded, "We just don't like him!"

I said, "Fine, if you don't like him, but if you ever place hands on him again the school, the police, or your mommas won't be able to save you. Do you understand exactly what I'm saying to you?"

To my shock they said, "Yes, ma'am," and walked away just as quickly as they had ran up to my car. When I walked back to the car I felt my body about to collapse as it was coming down from the rush. I sat there and wept and cried out to God thanking Him for protecting me and my children.

Draw close to God and He will draw close to you.
—James 4:8 NLT

After returning home I went to my office and cried some more and sat very still. I said to God, "Please, help me. I need you. I don't know what to do, where to turn. Who can help me?" I sat and waited yet I heard nothing. I got up from my desk and knelt down before God and asked Him to forgive me for anything I had done knowingly or unknowingly contrary to His teaching. I asked Him to forgive me for lashing out at Him and for placing other things and other people before Him. I asked Him to forgive my transgressions and there had been plenty while I dealt with my frustrations, sadness, and discontent while living in New Jersey. It would take another book to tell of all the wrong and spiteful decisions I made while living in a place I detested. When you are outside of the will of God, the devil knows how to take advantage of your isolation.

Shortly after crying out and asking God to forgive me, I prayed this prayer *by Stormie Omartin:*

Jesus, I invite you to be Lord over every area of my life today. I especially pray that You will be Lord over my children, marriage, finances, and friendships. I submit those areas of my life to You and ask You to reign in every way. I want You to be in control, not me. Just as Your disciples recognized that You are Lord, so do I acknowledge that You are Lord over all (John 13:13). Help me to love You as my Lord and Savior with all my heart, with all my soul, and with all my mind, just as You commanded in Your Word (Matthew 22:37). Help me to trust in You, Lord with everything that is within me and not to try and figure out life on my own (Proverbs 3:5).

Jesus, You once questioned why people called You Lord and yet didn't do what You asked them to do (Luke 6:46). Help me to always show evidence of Your Lordship in my life by living in obedience to Your ways and laws. Be Lord over my mind, thoughts, attitude, and emotions. Be Lord over my work, finances, giving, and spending. Be Lord over the way I use my time. Be Lord over my relationships, marriage, and my children. Be Lord over my health, habits, and words I speak. Be Lord over my dreams, fears, and future. I proclaim You Lord over my life.

In Jesus name, I pray.

Sometimes God speaks to us through a message we hear or a passage we read in a book and it lifts us up and encourages our soul when we need it most. I had been treating God as if He existed simply to be at my beck and call. God took me back to the place I used to be before I started begging and pleading to have my way.

When I arose from prayer I felt a fire on the inside that had become dim after moving to New Jersey. I could now hear God's voice again. He said, "Cheryl, sit down and type what I say and only send to who I instruct you to."

In the subject line of the email I typed: Urgent Prayer Request. I explained the bullying situation and the impact it was having on my son and our family. I asked everyone to pray that we be removed from the situation somehow and some way. You see, I learned early on, some people like it when they think you are struggling and miserable. So you have to be careful who you are transparent with and who you ask for prayer. After pressing the send button I thanked God and slept peacefully that night. I was so thankful to be back where I knew I belonged—in the will of God.

God answered our prayers quickly. The ringleader that assaulted my son pulled a knife on another boy the very next day and was arrested and expelled from the school. Within 24 hours after I surrendered to God he saved my son from trouble.

Surrender your whole being to Him to be used for righteous purposes.
                                        –Romans 6:13b (TEV)

After receiving my son's call with the news of how God answered our prayers, I remember crying and shaking uncontrollably—thankful this ordeal was behind us, yet thinking that could have been my child. I explained to my son that I didn't pray for that young man to be arrested, I just didn't want him around anymore, or to do even greater harm to someone else.

Lesson: Answered prayers bring us closer to God. I prayed and talked to God the rest of the day. I had a renewed sense of purpose. I was no longer comfortable just sitting in a pew and not serving God fully and completely so I became actively involved in the church. I was on fire for Jesus! I went from complaining every day to extending myself to other women and sharing the truths God had been pouring into me. I was learning how to love God more through His Word and by reading spiritual books. I could hear God saying dig deeper you have more to learn. Of course, I didn't want to hear that. There was a part of me still wanting to do things my way, and I would soon discover I had a lot more to learn about God and about myself.

We never know who we will encounter each day. As I went on my daily walks, I would see this woman who lived down the hill from me. I was typically so wrapped up in myself—I really didn't want to be bothered. But one day I stopped and introduced myself. We quickly hit it off and it wasn't long before we were discussing partnering in a business where we would do mental health assessments for companies. I didn't pray about the friendship or the business, I jumped in head first to partner with someone I barely knew. In retrospect, I realize I was trying to fill a void that only God could fill. I thought friendships, or going into business, would somehow fill the emptiness I felt inside. Later I learned it was a big mistake.

Things started to get interesting as we were moving through the process of setting up the incorporation for the business and we were looking for space. I felt so excited and exhilarated to be getting back into the career world. I had given up a thriving career as a personal shopper so that my husband could advance in his career. But this new business endeavor was my opportunity to do something for me again. Sometimes we ignore the warning signs that God sends our way because we want *something: status, material possessions, significance.*

I noticed my business partner demonstrating severe mood swings, changes in the information provided about the business and major expenditures without my regard or input. I let it go and excused it by saying, "God, I know You brought this to me." Actually, He was saying, "STOP" and I was saying, "GO."

When God blesses you there is no sorrow attached to it
—Proverbs 10:22b

If it's God, things will fall into place and be decent and in order. The opportunity I perceived to be on the up and up was simply a counterfeit blessing. I knew the moment when God released me to my own devices. We were all set for business and a church member called in a favor for us to get an appointment for a possible contract. I was so happy. As we were preparing for the meeting I could see something was wrong with my business partner. She became rude with the person we were meeting with, speaking in a condescending manner and making the person feel extremely uncomfortable.

My business partner abruptly ended the meeting saying she had to go take care of her dogs. We ended the meeting and I went home crying, trying to make sense of what had happened. The contact from the church was livid and asked me not to contact her again, and asked me if I was 'running a game.' I was dumbfounded and stayed in bed for two weeks, depressed. I couldn't believe how quickly the dream dashed. I prayed and the Holy Spirit instructed me to look up Bipolar disorder. When I did, she fit the description. I had seen the signs all along, but chose to ignore them. I felt so stupid for dishonoring God by not listening.

For everyone looks out for their own interests, not those of Jesus Christ.
—Philippians 2:21

I called the contact at church and shared my findings with her. We prayed for my business partner and I ceased all contact. I kept saying, "God, why didn't I listen!" And, I heard clearly, "You didn't trust Me when I told you to wait. You want to do things your way so now you have to suffer the consequences."

"When will man understand that God is in control?"
—Cheryl Polote Williamson

At this point I turned my attention and myself totally to God and He became my focus. I read, I prayed, and I cried. I prayed for others *intentionally and by name.* I asked God if He would find a way for me to get back to Texas, if it was HIS will.

Trust in the Lord with all your heart, and do not rely on your own understanding. In all your ways acknowledge Him and He will make your paths smooth.

–Proverbs 3:5,6 GW

Here I sit writing from Texas. God answered my prayer and opened a door for my husband's company to transfer us back. I was thrilled! It was a smooth transition and it was as if we had never moved away. We reconnected with our friends and church family, our children were happy, and we got the house we wanted to be in. I started serving in my church, hosting prayer groups in my home, and God even allowed me to open several new businesses.

Our boxing clubs are a place where women can come worship and workout at the same time. I've also written and released a book all in total devotion and obedience to God. Has the road to happiness and success been easy? NO! It's important to know that when you are on fire for Jesus; when you're working for Him, and taking discipline seriously and passionately, the devil will come after you with everything in his arsenal. I suppose the enemy realized that I was slipping out of his grip so he wondered, "What can I do to crush her spirit? How can I make her doubt God and turn away from Him—curse Him? How can I get her to stop praising Him altogether?"

Just as I was busy enjoying life in Texas and thinking my worse storms were all behind me, my faith was about to be tested like never before. The devil set a trap for me and started by using my son.

My son started getting into legal problems and making very poor decisions. This broke my heart, yet I kept praising God, sharing my story to help others, and digging deeper into God's Word.

It was tough, yet my faith remained intact and I began to get stronger. Although I was upset with my son I prayed with him, for him, and over him every day. I refused to allow the enemy to steal my joy or my child. When that didn't work the devil decided to bring out the big guns. He said, "Who can I use to destroy who she is in Christ, block her witness, and shut her down completely? Who is she close to? Who does she trust and wouldn't suspect?"

Just as the Bible says, God can use anyone, well, so can the devil. Just as Judas betrayed Jesus with a kiss, your *Judas is close enough to kiss you.* The devil used someone I called a friend for thirteen years to try to destroy my family, my business, and my reputation. She also attempted to turn my children against me all because she decided to allow herself to be used as a tool in the enemy's hand. My very own hairstylist plotted against me for years. She deceived me, lied to me, and gossiped about me to my friends. I opened up my heart to this woman. When I was praying for her marriage, she was actually preying on mine.

For many months I had to convince myself daily to choose Jesus over going to jail. I had friends telling me to do this or that— all which would have landed me in jail and bring no glory to God. ***Choose to listen to God carefully and allow Him to direct your every move.***

Every time I wanted to get back at my betrayer I would hear God whisper, "She will reap all she has sown—vengeance belongs to ME."

There were many days when I didn't want to wait on God to handle the situation. The pain of being betrayed by someone who called themselves my friend for more than a decade was more than my heart could bear. It took me a long time to realize I was in spiritual warfare. I wasn't fighting a human being—I was fighting a demon and Satan himself. And Satan comes to steal, kill, destroy, and block us from our purpose and destiny.

I was determined that Satan would not win. I surrounded myself with true prayer warriors that poured the Word of God over my family and me for months. I had my home and business blessed to usher out demonic spirits which had entered to destroy God's daughter. I stayed very close to God and allowed Him to fight the battle. Let me tell you something, when God fights for you—your victory is assured.

I did everything I could to shift myself in the right direction. I wrote my thoughts and feelings in a journal each day. I exercised to help me physically and emotionally. I went to counseling and started encouraging and empowering other women with the lessons I had learned. I cut contact with the woman who betrayed me and with those who were really not for me. I've discovered the closer your walk with the Lord, the smaller your circle. Not everyone deserves a front row seat in your life.

Through it all, God kept me. Today my business is thriving. I'm a public speaker, and I'm also writing two other books, and being a blessing to other women who are being challenged. I'm also actively engaged in helping make disciples for Christ.

Forgiveness is a powerful thing. It's really about you not the people who hurt you.

Once you forgive, the perpetrator's hold on you is broken. Your heart is free to love wholly and completely. If the devil knew the woman I would be after the storm he would never have come after me. God will take what the world perceives as your darkest hour and turn it into your greatest testimony.

My experiences have left me rooted and grounded in God's word, and I am determined to live for Jesus and continue to let go and let God have His way in my life. I'm determined to live in His will, and it's all for His glory!

12 Wisdom Keys to Shift You In the Right Direction:

- Always keep God first in your heart.
- Remain humble before God and be quick to repent.
- Examine your motives for everything you desire to do.
- Pray over every relationship and business endeavor before entering into it.
- Only God can fill a void in your life. He allows the void for the purpose of drawing you closer to Him.
- Be watchful of who you open up to or vent to. Discernment is vital.
- Imitation is not always flattery. Sometimes it's a sign that someone is coveting your life and identity.
- Don't extend yourself to everyone. Just because your heart and motives are pure towards someone doesn't mean that person's heart and motives are pure towards you.
- Pay attention to your intuition and the still small voice of the Holy Spirit. If we pay close attention we will know when God is trying to warn us of something.
- Forgive those who wrong you so that you can free yourself up.
- Love those who are difficult to love, even if you have to love them from afar.
- Keep moving forward especially when you don't feel like going on. Weeping may endure for a night, but joy comes in the morning.

ONCE YOU OWN IT, YOU CAN CONQUER IT

BY VAUGHNCHETTE RUDISILL

You either walk inside your story and own it or you stand out-
side your story and hustle your own worthiness.

–Brene Brown

This journey called life has so many twists, turns, potholes, and dead ends. All of it gets us where we need to be when it's all said and done.

Vaughnchette. Now that's an interesting name created by a 15-year-old mother who had no clue how she would do at this thing called mothering. My childhood and teen years were not exciting and I often found myself angry. I would smile even though I was hurt and worried about everything and everyone. I remember a time when I was around 8 or 9 years old and I could hear my mother being beat by one of my stepdad's. She was pleading to not be hit yet he was still hitting her. I could literally hear the slaps and shoves through the wall. We lived with my granny at the time and I wondered why no one ever intervened. I felt helpless and angry. I was scared that she would eventually be killed.

It took her 10 years to walk away. How can you love my mother, yet beat the hell out of her? This felt like a never-end-ing nightmare on repeat. Couple this with some former lovers and family members who felt that molesting children was the way to get their sexual needs met. It all had strong impact on the way I viewed men and how I viewed relationships as a whole. What it taught me is that I had better get really good at protecting myself and setting boundaries or else I would continue to bear the brunt of others poor decisions and lack of self-control. When I was young my mother would tell us, "Don't trust anyone ever." Meanwhile, in school we were being taught to "trust until you are given a reason not to." Which way was right?

Today I can embrace my "Jabez" name. If you're not familiar, Jabez was a baby in the Bible born out of his mother's pain. Jabez is actually the word for pain in Hebrew. So, when my mom had me, she was in so much pain, she just made up my name… Vaughnchette. After all, at fifteen what does anyone truly know? The tears still flow to this day because my mom made the deliberate choice to allow me to come into the world knowing that it meant life for her would change forever. I was the byproduct of a 15-year-old girl who was madly in love with an older, married man on active duty in the US Navy. He had no intentions of ever leaving his world to join ours.

Early on I got glimpses of forbidden relationships and the scars they leave on your life. I was born in 1976, prematurely weighing about one pound. The doctors were unsure if I would make it, being so tiny and sickly. I was diagnosed from birth with asthma and it kept my mother in the emergency room. My childhood was one of limited exposure as many elements triggered an asthma attack, from pollen to humidity.

Mom overcame unbelievable circumstances from withstanding abusive boyfriends and spouses, to demonstrating how to be loving and forgiving. Even when her needs were overlooked by family who showed favor to siblings who were more successful. She taught me how to stand tall when folks with "higher social status" tried to look down on me or expected me to jump through hoops for a chance to be around them. I cannot recall a time that my mother wasn't working to provide for my brother and I. With no high school education, she worked overtime and did not shy away from any challenge whether that was how to cover a double shift with minimal sleep or make a meal with minimal ingredients. She showed me what it meant to work hard even when your body is exhausted and you were not sure where the next meal was coming from. It was drilled into us that we must take care of our responsibilities even if the outcome would be painful.

Mom instilled within me that my black was indeed beautiful, even if no one noticed but me. Now that I am a parent, I have used storytelling to teach my own children important life lessons. We often forget that learning is also happening through observation no matter what our words are, the actions are being watched and translated in our children's minds. Seeing so many relationships begin and end at various stages in my life taught me to never fear starting over with anything. You quickly learn that both people and situations can change in an instant and your sanity must be of the utmost importance. My relationship with God was always a part of my journey even when I tried to kick him off the road because I felt I knew best. I learned from her that whatever you speak over yourself is what will be, so watch your mouth and thoughts. After all, you could not possibly expect someone else to build you up if you don't build yourself up.

Childhood and teen years were some of the most turbulent and unsure times of my life. When I entered the world as the child of a single mom, I learned quickly that there was always something she had to do or somewhere that she needed to be. My mother was rarely unemployed and she didn't believe in worrying about a job. She would often say, "Baby it's already done. It's just a matter of when I start." I can remember thinking, *How is it that she never worries about a job and she did not even graduate high school?* I neglected to mention that my mother's eyesight was so poor she was considered legally blind yet she worked, drove, and loved to calculate numbers.

Today, I can appreciate my mother, but growing up, I took so much for granted. I didn't realize when I was younger that we all had a choice of making the right decisions. The average person does not intend to make choices that hurt others. Some of the decisions my mother made simply didn't work out. I assumed that my mother knew the next route to take, but she didn't! She was feeling her way just like so many of us, and no way was she going to get it right each time. She too had to learn how to properly handle her anger and frustrations. I was angry at most of her mate choices because they impacted me. I wondered how she could have missed the signs. This guy was looking me up and down and he was supposed to be with my mom. Yet she gave him priority status, or worse yet, a key.

I was angry that more time was not taken to vet these men. Then the ones that appeared to be good prospects were boring and my mom had no interest in them long term. I often grimaced inside and thought, *He seemed normal.* The nights my mom worked late were the worst for me. These were often the times when sick relatives and mom's boyfriends were intent on violating me since they knew I was home alone. "Come here CeeCee, and sit on Uncle's Lap." "You sure are a pretty chocolate child." These are words I dreaded because I knew they would be followed by hands reaching under my dress…sometimes even in a room full of people. No one noticed the improperly placed hands and I felt I could not trust anyone much less tell what was happening.

My introduction to sex was molestation. I would hear sly comments like, "Hey, when your mom leaves, you know what's up." I tried to smile through the anger yet I would not dare share it with my mom. She was already working so hard to provide and give us a decent place to live. I would not dare add to the stress or take away from her momentary happiness. When I was 13 years old I had anxiety to the point where I had a mini stroke, and a portion of my mouth drooped for a while.

There did come a time when I shared what had happened, but because I was caught in my own promiscuity my mother didn't believe me until well into my adult years. I would often run away from home but still attend school.

I have spent a lot of time sharing stories about my molestation but I haven't shared about my mother's anger issues and inability to use restraint during discipline. Whippings were full-on beat downs. I was whipped with extension cords, wire hangers, brooms, lamps, and anything else within reach. She often got her point across by hitting, yelling, and throwing objects, so whenever she had one of her episodes I would run away—or I would run away knowing an episode was on the way because of something I had done. Mom would have to confirm the frequency but I at a minimum ran away monthly if not more often for a good year or so. I would stay gone anywhere from one to five nights. At the same time even though I was angry and running away, I would still try to keep an eye on my mom from afar because more often than not she was being physically and emotionally abused by her current mate.

One time I stopped by our apartment to check on my mom. I hadn't gone far and unbeknownst to her I saw her leave for work each day. I was literally an apartment unit down the walkway. This particular time I stopped in and the jerk she was dating, and later married, snatched off her hairpiece and used scissors to cut off her false nail tips. I was mortified and horrified that a person could do this to my mother! I asked myself, *Would he have tried that if I were home with her?* Even as a runaway I was still trying to keep an eye on home happenings. It was no wonder my nerves were not right.

When I ran away, I'd end up at a stranger's place to get myself cleaned up. Sometimes they were angels, other times I was in enemy territory and wondered if this time would be the time I didn't make it back home. A defining moment happened when I was about 14 years old. One night after a typical mother/daughter run-in, I left home walking and knocked on the wrong motel room door. I don't even remember what made me walk to that motel lot except there seemed to be a lot of activity and folks were out drinking, smoking, and laughing. It seemed like fun. After all, I was ready to be grown, so I thought. I was so tired and cold that I knocked on this door at the end of corridor and a gray haired older man answered the door. The room was dark, muggy, and smelled of old dirty carpet. He called me his "Teddy." I didn't make it to school that entire week. The guy brought food in each day and for the life of me I don't know why I didn't run when he was in the bathroom or when he left to run an errand—I just stayed. He didn't hold me hostage but for some reason I was completely immobilized. I looked at the ceiling one of the times he was enjoying himself on top of me, thinking, *How did I get here? Why didn't I just stick it out at home? This wasn't a better alternative. Now what do I do?* Home... the place where I worried about being sexually molested as a child and now here I was in a situation just as bad. What had I become?

This motel experience changed me. It would be the final time I would run away. Something within me clicked and said you have to stop this and get on with your life. The next time may be your last.

My classmates on the other hand were busy living their lives, going to games, doing teen stuff and I was worrying about my mother's and anyone else's burdens. I could fix them or so I thought.

Every decision my mom made had an impact on me. Even though she is sorry for mistakes, she still has to live with her decisions and so do I.

Some decisions are freeing but you can be stuck with the bad ones forever.

Because I did not feel safe in my own home environment I learned to distrust everyone until they proved trustworthy. In whatever relationship I entered, I learned to guard my heart and expect disappointment.

Growing up, I wondered if anyone was actually who they said they were. Is anyone actually comfortable with who they are and able to resist making things up to make themselves sound great? That was the beginning of Lady V—learning to love herself, flaws and all. As a child you often think, just wait until I am an adult. I will make all my own choices and they will be the right ones too. No one is going to tell me what to do.

Funny thing about adulthood, it's on you. You can blame someone else but when it all boils down to it, it's all on you. The healing for me to write this chapter is being able to "own" all that comes with me and all that comes as a result of being me. Society likes to talk about owning in terms of real estate and businesses but they rarely talk about owning choices, decisions, and consequences. No one wants to face the dialogue that needs to happen with self to truly grow.

I was married twice before marrying the absolute love of my life. Now you may say, "Wow, twice married and on the third." Yes, that's right, the third time was indeed the charm! I am not about to give a litany of excuses as to why the other two marriages didn't work but I am going to talk with you about the danger of not knowing self. If you don't know yourself then you will walk through all kinds of doors and relationships that are not for you. You will hurt a lot of people along the way if you don't face who you are and get a handle on what you are seeking. Who are you when there is no one to say, "Amen" or "You can do it." Who are you when there is no ram in the bush? Who are you when there is no Mac, Mary Kay, or Clinique to cover up your blemishes? When you get home you have to deal with the real person. First you deal with you then the other people you're in a relationship with, mates, spouses, family members and friends. It's important that we all have at least one person with who we can feel comfortable revealing every pimple, wrinkle, extra pound, every internal eye rolling behind our smiles. You should be able to talk about your expectations and disappointments as well. It's wonderful to have someone there for you as you battle nightmares from your childhood every night. Until I could get there, I had to spend some time with Vaughnchette. There was no way I would have been able to have a healthy relationship or even recognize one when it was staring me in the face if I hadn't made some real changes in my life.

My shift happened at the close of marriage number two when I was explaining to my former spouse my reasons for moving on. I didn't want to continue being with someone who didn't understand me and all I had gone through and where I was headed. I could not believe I actually used the "It's not you, it's me" excuse. It was true though; my junk was my own and it was heavy and smelly.

I began to journal about my process and when something caused me pain or caused me to feel less than who I know I was born to be, I knew it was time for a change. What is it you are actually seeking? Is it external or internal? Instead of always asking what the other person wanted and how could I please them I had to figure out what I wanted and who I was. Was I just existing on this earth or was there something more?

With two failed marriages under my belt, I had these two amazing little children that had to walk that path with me, and they experienced hurt as a result of my not being quick enough to "own my junk." Tenice and Mark are both now serving in the US Navy but they will both tell their own stories one day of how they lived thru momma's decisions. They loved me through the season of: "we are moving out of state, no clue where we will live and we will just start at this Ramada Inn in Norfolk and go from there." I thought back to the day that I moved from Georgia to Virginia and wondered for the hundredth time what I could have been thinking. All I had with me were my two and three year old babies, our personal effects, and a few toys. What was I thinking when I married the next person who was the opposite of the first husband? That meant it had to work, right? What was I thinking when I thought you simply say what you want to say, when you want to say it, and ignore the consequences? It's the truth. So just say it. How wrong I was. Every choice yields a consequence. Every choice has an impact and when walking through life, it's best to recognize this up front before speeding forward with no brakes. You will hit something.

When you don't take the time to pause, you can expect to make your journey a lot more difficult than it needs to be. I am not of the traditional mindset and did not have a desire to go to college, get a degree, get married, and have the white house with the picket fence, two well behaved kids, and a dog. I chose the military instead. But I had asthma and I knew that it would stop me from having a career and eventually retiring from the military. I had to put homeownership and the dog on hold for a while. I decided to start a business instead. My process was completely the opposite of what society teaches. It is okay to dare to be different. God still creates priceless masterpieces even with flawed materials.

The path of life is paved with a thousand options; the most important is to make sure your path is aligned with God and not to allow your fears to make you immobile. Were it not for my faith, I am positive I would be in a mental health facility. There were times that I wondered if I should at least arrange an overnight stay because I was afraid there was no way I could get through what I was facing.

I couldn't have survived on my own. I had to learn to trust and build relationships as part of the healing process.

Even when I thought I was flying solo there were people in the background holding me up. The next time you are tempted to believe that life is a one woman or one man show, just think about all the people who are involved in your process.

As we move forward, there are some lessons I learned along the way that helped make the journey tight but still right.

Lesson One: Allowing yourself to be misused or abused is not okay. You have another choice. Walk Away. Get Out. You are too valuable for anything less.

Lesson Two: There are warning signs to caution you of what's ahead should you continue on the same course.

Lesson Three: Mental Health is so important and when you are not sure how to make sense of it all, don't be afraid to talk to someone. Seek help because keeping it all inside isn't healthy.

Lesson Four: You have a choice as to how you spend your time and resources.

Lesson Five: Choose your friends wisely, for your life may depend upon the choice.

It took me over thirty years to learn who I could and could not trust, and I still miss it sometimes especially if it "feels" like the relationship should work. I learned that just because someone stands beside you they are not necessarily with you. It doesn't mean they are cheering for you. It could mean they are simply there for the overflow of blessings.

Once I learned how to properly organize the people in my life, I gained traction and released a ton of frustration. I learned to really pay attention to the actions of others where it concerned those I loved or me. Some people were with me when I was in a stronger financial position because they knew I would give of my last to ensure they had what they needed. When the roles were reversed and calls became less frequent I got the message loud and clear that I was temporary. I discovered that the people I really wanted to have in my life were those who stuck around even when I had nothing.

I became a lot less angry and I got real comfortable with the word "no" both saying and hearing it. The word "no' isn't always comfortable. It often stings and rarely is appreciated. "No" is such a powerful word and is often used in both establishing and maintaining boundaries.

- No, I will not lower my standards to accept your treatment as I value me more.
- No, I choose to not say exactly what I am thinking as I am accountable for my words once I allow them loose into the atmosphere.
- No, I love you for you and not for what you can do for me
- No, I cannot allow your issue to become my burden

I've heard Oprah say that you have to teach people how to treat you.

Funny thing is, you cannot teach others how to treat you, if you don't know how to treat yourself. How do you greet yourself in the morning or at night? Do you note that you see bags under your eyes, extra love dimples on the thighs, or do you say to self, "Good morning, let's do this!"? My personal favorite is, "Get those chompers brushed and put on the best thing you will ever wear Lady V—your smile." I also say, "This situation is not a surprise to God even if it's shocking the hell out of me!"

Until I learned how to treat myself, I had no clue how to govern myself with others and I didn't set healthy boundaries. Before I learned to value me, I remember thinking to myself, *What I have to say about marriage is irrelevant because I have been married twice and on my third. No one will listen to me.* I had a lot of life and business experiences but no college degree so what could I teach anyone? Those type of self-defeating thoughts are what stops businesses from being birthed, books from being written, prevents some from sharing their story and others from walking through the doors of opportunity. The things we speak to ourselves are either dream killers or dream birthers. Don't waste energy comparing and contrasting your life with others. No more comparing zip codes, skin tone, educational goals, dress size, income level, vehicle types, etc. We have a destiny and no one can take it from us.

There is a quote by Eleanor Roosevelt that says, "No one can make you feel inferior without your permission." The magic happens when we recognize that no one is in control of how we feel and speak except us.

Owning my truth and my story leaves me with the power to rise above. Owning my truth and my story frees me from the tendency to blame other people for my shortcomings. Owning my truth and my story allows me to breathe in and out even when labored. Owning my truth and my story gives me the confidence to look in the mirror and say, "You did well!"

My life is far from perfect but I can now put things in perspective and almost tell my story without shedding tears.

Momma, I thank you for teaching me so many important lessons. Every day I think about the choice you made to allow my birth in spite of you being labeled an uneducated teen. I'm thankful I can hear your voice of reason any time I want. It's taken years but owning my truth and my story has made me a survivor and given me a chance to move forward as I write a new chapter.

THE SHIFT THAT UNLEASHED THE GIFT

MARQUITA MILLER

"Complacency is the enemy of success."

–Brandon Eley

M y father was an entrepreneur and told my siblings and me that if we had a choice of selling ice in Alaska or working for someone who sells it, always choose the first choice so you can control your ability to create the life you desire.

My husband and I taught our children to appreciate owning their own businesses as well. They have had vending machines, made jewelry, and tried all sorts of ventures, all to instill the mantra my family follows: it's not about where you go to work, it's about what you're going to own. The key to running successful businesses starts with answering one question. Is there a need for what you're asking consumers to pay for?

I started Five Star Tax and Business Solutions to help people start, grow, and connect their business by offering accounting, payroll services, tax preparation, business startup, and consulting.

But let's go back a few years. When I was 15 and still living at home, after filing my income taxes at H&R Block I got a big refund and I was on top of the world. What I didn't realize was that I claimed myself even though I was living at home. When my dad,

115

a business owner, recognized my mistake, he told me not only did I have to amend the taxes, I also had to pay the money back. This sent two messages to me. The first one was that a mistake that I made had an impact on many more people than myself. And two, even though doing things right might not yield an initial gain, it's better than having to pay a penalty down the road for doing things the wrong way. When I returned to H&R Block to figure out how to amend my taxes, I was prepared to have to pay them for their services. Thankfully, the woman didn't charge me. Instead, she gave me a publication that showed me what I would have to do to properly file. I went home, read it, did the paperwork, and walked back to H&R Block. The woman was so impressed, she offered me a job there. I didn't work for them long because I quickly discovered I could work for myself doing taxes for friends and family. My talent was transportation to my purpose. We all have talents and gifts. It's up to us to discover how they can be useful to someone.

In 2000, I left a good paying job to launch my company. I rented a tiny office space in an area where I had access to various types of clients: old money—people who could afford to pay a lot of money for the service I offered, but probably didn't need them, and check-to-check folks—people who wanted and needed a rapid refund. My husband passed out flyers and put them on cars, and I talked to everyone I ran into about my tax services. I did 300 tax returns the first year.

Know Your Clientele

It wasn't long before I'd outgrown my 300-square foot office but I can't underestimate the benefits of that location. It was in the same building as the Boys and Girls Club, so there was a constant influx of mostly single parents coming in and out and they were the ones who needed tax preparation/rapid returns the most.

I soon rolled out phase two of my business, which served under-cover business owners, people who hadn't filed/were afraid to file/didn't know they were supposed to file. Many were not legally set up as businesses and needed to be educated. I gained their trust and their business.

Think Long Term

When tax season was over, I still had to pay rent. By now I had moved from an office that was $200 a month to a larger space that cost $500 per month. I had to aggressively seek out people who needed to become legitimate business owners by showing them how and why they needed to take their businesses to the next level, all while I was doing the same for my business.

Don't Give It Away

For a while I offered free consultations, which turned out to be a huge mistake. People were lined up to talk to me for free about what I could do for their businesses. But that's really all they were willing to do was talk. They didn't value my time and they were devaluing what I had to offer. Eventually, I charged a small amount to set up an LLC (Limited Liability Company). The business was growing but there were some very lean months. There were days I would cry because some of the clients would not pay. I learned to ask God for exactly what I needed. When rent was due I asked Him for $500. This wasn't an entrepreneurial journey it was a spiritual journey!

Eventually all sorts of doors started to open. The Kansas City Black Chamber of Commerce president hired me and coached me on how to stop thinking like a mom and pop show and to learn to create different streams of income. One steady source of revenue was speaking engagements. I spoke everywhere about the importance of setting up LLC's: restaurants, churches, chamber events, you name it. When I was finished speaking, my husband would sign people up for consultations.

The key to most of it was to educate people about the importance of following the rules. There were so many people in business who were not familiar with the laws that could have a major impact on them if they were caught cutting corners. I once helped a woman get set up in a business doing a final clean on houses. It started because she was displaced from her home following a tornado and couldn't move back in until a final clean—no dust and debris present in the house. She realized she could do it herself but had to bid for the job. She was paid $2,000 to do a final clean on her own house. Other neighbors who were displaced heard about it so she did it for other people. The good news was she made a million dollars the first year. The bad news was her profit was only about $100,000. Like so many new business owners, she didn't know how to manage her company. She made three big mistakes:

1. She didn't understand the nature of the business and was unfamiliar with rules and regulations and ended up with lots of tax issues.
2. She didn't establish a plan for payroll and accounting.
3. She fell in love with big checks and didn't plan for the future.

Even when things were going great you have to always stop to examine the business side of your business. There are so many ways you can get in trouble with the IRS, Department of Labor, and Department of Revenue.

After many years of running a successful company, here are some other things I have learned:

1. You have to get an attitude that says N.O.W. (No Opportunity Wasted). Stop waiting to get in the race because you're already in there. It doesn't matter if you haven't been running. It doesn't matter if you are still at the starting line. What DOES matter at this very moment is that you get a fire that will cause you to run at your fastest potential. Let me be clear—you are not competing against

your friends, neighbors, siblings, church members, people on social media, or any other individual. Your measuring stick is your God-given potential. Each of us has a purpose and a mission, which is to help other people. You have something so great on the inside of you and you have to share it with the world. You are carrying around a solution to a problem that millions of people need to hear or experience. When will you get started?

2. You can have excuses or you can have results but you cannot have both. When will you stop making excuses? There is somebody that will take your worst day and praise God for it. When I had the privilege of traveling to Haiti, I experienced things that altered my complaining. Patients were outside the largest hospital pending medical treatment to only be faced with the fact that one out of two ER patients would die just waiting to be seen. Now tell me—what was your excuse again? You don't have the funding to unleash your dream. That big fat lie is straight from the pit of hell. At this very moment you have everything you need to move yourself to the next level if you will only get started. Stop the excuses and be determined to obtain some results. You don't need the money until you need the money. In other words—get started with what you already have.

Once again I can confirm the results in this method: Every time I've started a journey and couldn't quite see my way to the end, God revealed more pieces and provision as I moved down the line. There are resources you will never need or have unless you get started. I think it's a fair assumption to say God won't waste the provision on a person who is not committed to the vision.

3. It's time to deal with the four-letter word that keeps people stuck before they can get started. This word causes people to not ask the question they know they want to ask. This word has caused many people to miss providential appointments. FEAR! The reality is most of our fears come from the perceived threat. We fear what people *may* say. We fear the *possibility* of failure. We fear the *what ifs*: What if my book isn't good? What if no one patronizes my business? What if my voice cracks when I start my song? All these what ifs! I am going to challenge you to replace fear with FAITH. Because, what if everything goes right? What if this chapter helps shift your life into high gear to experience some of your greatest successes? What if the positive outcomes happen? Be committed to shatter the fears that have held your life hostage. Be dedicated to releasing your faith.

I was supposed to have a simple "outpatient" surgical procedure. It turned into a surgery, which required four months of recovery! That seemed like foolishness to me, then and now, but God worked it all out for my good in the end. During my stay in the hospital, I helped two nurses start their own businesses. What those businesses had to do with changing my bandages I will never know. I call it purpose chasing you and finding you everywhere you go. What's chasing you? What opportunity keeps coming up over and over?

During my four months out of the office, my business revenue didn't skip a beat. That's because God allowed me to empower the employees that work for me. Early on I realized that choosing the right employees was crucial, especially the front lead because she was the first person representing my business, my brand, and me. I poured into her life for years and when I needed her most she was there. And so were other employees, part-time people who worked extra hours while I was down because they understood and believed in our mission to help people realize their dreams.

I can hear it like it was yesterday: "PECK, PECK, PECK" were the words the Bishop spoke as I viewed one of the nation's largest women's conferences via the Internet. The sermon, "Peck, Peck, Peck" was a series the Bishop preached on the importance of recognizing that there should be a structure and order to our lives. But that structure and order can only be achieved when we learn to focus on the right things. It cannot be rushed.

The "pecking order" is an agricultural term a psychologist first used when studying the behavior of chickens. Within the henhouse structure, the strongest hen ruled the roost. For the most part, that theory is used in human settings too. Whether in corporate America or your own company, one person is, and probably should be, in charge. If anything is to be run decently and in order, that leadership role shouldn't be taken lightly.

I could relate to this scenario all too well. I watched the live stream not because I couldn't afford the registration cost or travel package. It wasn't because I couldn't get off work to attend. I viewed it from my comfortable recliner because I had numerous staples holding my stomach together. I needed help to provide even the simplest care for myself including walking from one room to the next. It was a point in my life that was one of my most challenging.

A medical procedure that I was led to believe was pretty routine went wrong and what should have resulted in an overnight stay at the hospital at best turned into a week. I underwent major surgery and it took me months to get well. For an entrepreneur like me who was accustomed to ruling the roost when it came to my company, this was almost unbearable. Except that I had no other choice but to bear it. If you're ruling the roost, you'd better make sure the pecking order is correct and based not on outward appearances, friendship, politics, or even love. You need to be sure that people who are representing you in your absence are the best people for the job. That doesn't happen overnight. We never know how or when our gifts will be unleashed. Sometimes they will even be unleashed through someone else.

That moment was the last day I would remember living below my God-given potential. I no longer would allow life to just happen. I would no longer allow "NO" to stop me. I would no longer create a long list of excuses to explain the lack of results. I would no longer expect someone to save the day for me. And I would no longer take my purpose for granted. It's funny how four months of recovery time will allow you to come face to face with yourself.

My health crisis caused me to ask lots of questions: "Why me? How could this be happening to me? When can I get my old life back?" Believe me when you ask questions, eventually you will get answers. I recall the Bible scripture Mark 4:40 when the disciples woke Jesus up to ask Him, "Don't you care that we are perishing?" Jesus replied with two questions, "Why are you so afraid? Do you still have no faith?" The answers to my questions came to me in the same question form: "Why do you want to go back to your old life?"

Since I had a surplus of open time, I pondered the question for several days. My assessment period would reveal the strength of relationships, the density of my leadership, the degree of imbalance in my life, how purpose follows you wherever you go, and the untouched capacities of faith. The shift happened almost instantly on that conference night. I knew that God was using that conference host to speak to my spirit, foreshadow my future, and unfold my new life. That was in 2012 and I can tell you that my life is almost unrecognizable! The shift unleashed the gift.

I am now hosting one of the fastest growing business conferences, No More Excuses Only Results. This is an event that causes its attendees to get confrontational about their potential and success. I started hosting the conference before the 2012 shift but it had a new momentum. I would also become a contributing writer for Black Enterprise Magazine. That door would allow me the opportunity to interview a host of celebrities, VIPs, and small business owners all across the world. I would go on to publish more books and empowerment CDs. I was nominated and selected as one of the influential Women of Kansas City; one of the *Kansas City Business Journal's* "Women Who Mean Business" and became a member of Alpha Kappa Alpha Sorority. I would get invitations to speak across the United States about Entrepreneurship and I traveled to Haiti to teach my faith-based entrepreneurship seminar, "Faithpreneur". I share none of these accomplishments to boast but only to share my dedication and belief in entrepreneurship. It isn't something I picked up as an adult or even as a teen. It is something I was born into. And here is one thing I know for sure; if you want to learn about faith, start your own business.

Ask yourself what would you do for free or probably have done for free. I am here to tell you that the answer to that question is your mission field. It is time for you to unleash your gift into your greatness. Today is the last day you will remember living below your God given potential. You will no longer allow life to just happen. You will no longer take your purpose for granted. How many others will be blessed by your gift? How many will be denied if you keep it to yourself? My dad would say every day, ask yourself whether you're an asset or a liability. Are you adding value, or are you costing others? It's up to each of us to find the tools that will help us add financial prosperity to our lives. You CAN start a business. Will you?

BLACK BUTTERFLY

BY JENNIFER F. SMITH

"Nothing can stop God's Plan for your life."

–Isaiah 14:27

Imagine inadequacy, insufficiency, self-doubt, hurt, and depression transforming into discovery, renewal, faith, and healing. This describes me! It often looks easy but looks are deceiving. My shift has been one of clarity and understanding.

I was raised in a two-parent home but my parent's relationship was not perfect. There were constant arguments. I couldn't relate to the families like those on the Cosby Show and Family Matters, where the parents had conflicts, kissed, made up, and then sat for dinner.

I had hatred towards my dad because of the arguments with my mom. I often wondered if the fights were my fault at times. I couldn't share with anyone that I had thoughts of what it would be like if I never existed. I thought about suicide but never acted upon it. I attended Catholic school, which exposed me to religion but I didn't understand God. My religion gave me clear instructions that suicide was unacceptable, unless I wanted a guaranteed spot in hell. This was my earliest memory of struggle that would later develop into my gift to help others. From day one, God had a plan for me to share with others the beauty and pains of marriage, faith, forgiveness, and living a mentally healthy life. Life has a way of making your struggles develop your character whether you want it to or not. Growth happens from pain when you least expect it. And this was only just the beginning for me.

I didn't realize this concept until in my later 20s when I was married with a daughter. During my marriage, things were challenging. It was similar to what I experienced with my own parents but it wasn't always that way. My husband was my first real boyfriend because I wasn't allowed to date. We met my senior year of high school through a good friend. He was her boyfriend's best friend. The three happened to be at her house, bored, looking through her pictures when he came across mine and wanted to know who I was. Of course, my friend told him and called me. My future husband and I played on the phone like silly teenagers and eventually met in person. I couldn't have company so we stood in the hallway of my apartment building. He tried to kiss me and I wouldn't let him. He proclaimed, "You are going to be my wife."

We started dating after that day and went to my prom. He was a gentleman, picking me up in his car and saying, "Yes Ma'am" when speaking to my mother. All the good stuff you wanted in young love. He was there for my early college years when I resided on campus at University of Illinois-Chicago. He was there all the time and sat in the lecture halls with me. He majored in eating up my meal plan. Culturally diverse friends, great work study job, and Greek life opportunities were my focus until everything changed. Life would never be the same!

Pregnancy Test: pink plus sign. It was the summer before my junior year in college. I was pregnant and scared. My thoughts raced on how to fix this mess. Like in the TV series "Scandal," I turned into Olivia Pope. In order to "fix it" we decided to get an apartment, real jobs, and he eventually proposed marriage. I jumped in headfirst but no one ever explained that marriage takes work. Hard Work!

We were a young married couple. I didn't know much about being a wife. As a woman, I felt it was my responsibility to be the glue to keep our family together. I hated the feeling of failure, so I tried to make it work. I was already use to disappointment. I had a nice wedding but I missed out on the baby shower, engagement party, photoshoot, and honeymoon experiences. We were "babies" trying our hardest. Rent was expensive. I had bills like gas and water utilities that I never imagined before. I learned about priorities and those bills that you can live without, such as internet, cable, landline phone, etc. What's the saying, "you didn't realize your parents had a light bill until the lights got turned off."

While I finished undergraduate studies, my husband worked nights. We never saw each other and I was left with a crying baby while studying for midterms. My mother helped financially but that pride will get you. I didn't like taking money from her when I had a husband at home that should be providing for me. I wasn't credit savvy and used many credit cards intending to pay later only to find out I wouldn't have the money. One late payment could triple your payments, which I couldn't afford on my salary. Things were piling up and my husband wasn't the best with money. There would be negative balances even after a payday. This stress along with cooking, cleaning, and keeping it steamy in the bedroom daily was too much. My future did not look promising except for washing clothes and wiping noses. I didn't image the possibilities I could become if I dared to dream at the time. In the moment, I was going through a cycle of going to work, being a wife, taking care of my child, then repeat. I asked, "Why didn't anyone tell me that life could be this hard?" I could then see why my parents argued all the time.

Our schedules changed after I graduated and got a job teaching pre-kindergarten and a part-time cashier position. My husband began making good money. It seemed so easy for him with only a high school diploma. I felt inadequate because I struggled making half his salary with a degree. I changed careers and worked in child welfare, which had it limitations too. I said, "In order for me to get ahead, I have to make it happen with more paper." By this, meaning higher degrees. I wanted my household to be equal and bring my best share to the table. If my husband brought $50,000 a year with no degree, I wanted to bring that and more. He was not going to outshine me! I wanted to ensure our financial issues were not due to me not putting in the work. I made a choice to return to graduate school.

I started graduate school and learned my craft in counseling. This is when turmoil hit my marriage. I thought things were getting better when it spiraled downhill after only three years. We grew apart. He had dreams of being an entrepreneur using "get rich quick" schemes while I wanted it through hard work. This man did everything from selling vacuums, organizing spa and pamper parties, as well as going to truck driving school. He had the gift of gab and this eventually got him in trouble.

My husband developed a relationship with another woman. I didn't pay attention to the red flags. You know the ones: work 6 A.M to 3 P.M. but home at 8 P.M. smelling fresh and not hungry even though you cooked type of flag. What's done in the dark comes to light. The woman eventually came to my home to tell me about the affair. We made attempts with counseling and pastoral advice. He continued the relationship even after I forgave his indiscretion. Nothing could convince me after that to stay with him when he continued the affair.

One night we had a huge argument. There were actions and words exchanged that I wouldn't wish on anyone. The fight escalated into him hitting me in the face. He had never placed his hands on me. Ever! I was shocked and yes, I returned the gesture with help. I found the biggest knife and the rest was a blur. I thought my life was over and I was going to jail. We had turned into monsters.

I knew I deserved so much more than this. I was a ragdoll pulled between two worlds. Marriage in my eyes was about love and sacrifice, not one-sidedness and selfishness. It was about being supportive, caring, and building each other up. That was what every love story taught me. How could two people so in love now hate each other? I felt hurt and betrayed. It was the toughest decision of my life. How does one walk away from a marriage? Why didn't God fix this?

The day the divorce was finalized, my ex-husband walked out the courtroom with nothing to say to me. I was left with a nauseating feeling in my stomach. Was it over, or was this the beginning? It was the worst feeling. Had I done the right thing, or was this selfish? More importantly, had I disappointed God?

I reflected on the root of those thoughts. I carried this "F'd-up child" complex. Somehow over the years, I made up this crazy concept while observing my parents unhappiness and regretting not being the best role model to my younger sister. My mother wanted the best for me. Being the oldest is like being the guinea pig of "what not to do." I was pregnant at 19 years old, "shacked up" before marriage, and always in need of help. My sister had the opportunity to not make the same mistakes. She obtained two master's degrees and her own property while I was still trying to get my life right. I just couldn't get things right. I thought I was not a positive example for her. I laugh today because I said, "Oh Jenn, the lessons you'll learn," but that experience was disheartening. So, while going through my divorce, I remembered that feeling. Even in my perseverance, it still felt bad. I questioned, "How do I make this work?" I was a divorced, single parent, with major debt and at risk of dropping out of my master's program by 30 years old. The world was absolutely unfair.

I prayed and cried every night. Divorce has a stigma of "damaged goods" and "drama." Co-parenting was a headache. You cannot make a father do more than he is capable of doing. I had to make a choice whether all those things I feared was worth more than my self-worth and future. There were so many unhealthy relationships happening all around me, that I had to be a model for my daughter. I refused to be unhappy in my own home. I was determined to shift the puzzle pieces of life and make things fit. I received monetary help from my mother for bills, found affordable afterschool care, and made more economical meals because it was only the two of us. I made the effort to be a more transparent mom and talk to my daughter about lessons I learned a little too late. I wasn't ready to seek a relationship so I relied on friends for emotional support. Even though I was a single mother, a single woman, I knew I was not alone.

Even though I had gone through a divorce, I finished my master's degree program. I so excelled in my studies that my practicum professor encouraged me to continue within their doctoral program. I kindly declined because I was ready to move within my purpose of helping others heal from trauma. I knew the struggles from my past and the trauma I witnessed through my work. I didn't know at the time that I could be my own entrepreneur and philanthropist by helping young ladies not become teen mothers but birth purpose, encouraging fathers to be in their children's lives to demonstrate strength and leadership, helping educate young couples to take marriage seriously, and encouraging those to enjoy singlehood. I wanted to be a blessing to everyone that crossed my path. I had finally discovered a way to incorporate that into my career and daily life.

Single parenthood didn't appear that bad after the divorce but I was still human with needs. I enjoyed dating, even if it was with men with "Shit-u-ations." Yes! They had so much going on from having wives, fiancées, kids, or played games for sex. The attention was good.

My daughter had become a "latch-key" child. She would arrive home from school, do homework, cook her own dinner, and go to bed before I arrived home from work. I prayed daily that child protective services didn't come knocking at our door. I worked in child welfare and didn't want any parts of it. I hid some struggles from friends and family out of embarrassment and over time it became easy to do. I was depressed after being rejected three times for a home loan despite a credit score of 700. Lenders said I owed too many student loans with my low income. At night, I still felt so empty. So alone. Something was missing. Why was I feeling like this?

I had a nice apartment, two degrees, and making a way for myself. I thought the marriage was the issue but now that was gone. Before I was able to move forward, I had to do some soul healing. It takes a strong woman to realize that and let go of past hurt. You never fully know how free you can feel after letting go. In doing so, I really had to strengthen my relationship with God and learn about forgiveness if I was to continue to be blessed in my own projects. Things such as shopping, sex, working out, and eating great food could not fill that void. I realized, foremost, I had to ask for forgiveness in EVERYTHING!! First for myself. I had broken vows I had made in front of God. I still desired a healthy relationship later but wanted to be whole before doing so. I couldn't displace that hurt from all those life changes onto others. Lashing out because I had "issues" was not going to be helpful. I couldn't blame anyone but me.

I had to forgive the things I'd done on those nights that I was angry with my dad for arguing with my mom. I had to accept that no marriage is perfect. I could not take personally the things people did to me. There was a higher power that loved me. And in that love, I can grow and give back the lessons learned.

Shortly after graduation, I found myself counseling within a pregnancy prevention program in Englewood. It is known as one of the roughest neighborhoods on the south side of Chicago. Pregnancy Prevention: How ironic. I never worried about the shootings or impoverishment in the area. My purpose was to work with those youth. I'd always wanted an opportunity to let my creativity run wild and I was able to develop my own programs. I started a mentoring group called "Girls Group," which provided a safe space to talk about issues such as sex, drugs, and relationships. This is where I started "Little Misses", introducing the girls to healthy eating, table etiquette, and empowerment of each other. I'd come to learn that it was difficult for young girls to compliment each other without thinking jealousy or homosexuality.

My pride and joy was the "Boys-n-Books" Club that I developed. As a woman, I cannot teach a man to be a man. I can provide a safe space for them to flourish. Many of our young black boys will not read a book. What's the phrase? *If you want to hide something, put it in a book.* I believe our black boys are limited in resources because there are so many programs for girls. These girls become strong, independent women in a world of men still "discovering themselves" in their 40's because no one planted the seed. I plan to make that change. Helping youth and families is where I belong. These programs developed the foundation for my future dream: my nonprofit organization. Nothing is limiting this but ME!

> *"The future belongs to those who believe in the beauty of their dreams."*
>
> —Eleanor Roosevelt

Just when you think the storm is over, life will grab you by the hand, shake things up, and make sure you're paying attention. I was dreaming of becoming a licensed counselor and starting my own non-for profit organization when my grandmother fell ill with dementia. My grandmother was my life. She knew things about me that no one knew. She was on a fixed income but always found a way to give to others. She was love. So when she became ill, it was heartbreaking. You are never fully prepared even after playing it over and over in your mind. She stayed strong even through admittance to the nursing facility. I will never forget our last real conversation where she told me she was ready and reflected on how short life was. She knew death was near. I could feel the "If I could've done things differently" energy flow from her body. She had regrets. If she could, she would have changed many things in her life. I changed the day she passed away. I will never forget, October 2, 2013. I looked out the window and let the sun hit my face. I said goodbye with a smile. She was free and I was to be her legacy. I will live with no regrets. This was it! It was time to move full speed ahead in being the boss in everything in my life. Life is too short!

After my grandmother's death, I gave my life over to the service of others. In preparation for my own future organization, I first wanted to give back and support others. I needed to build my network. I became a volunteer "hog," devouring every opportunity I could find. I started with Chicago Cares, an organization that leads projects all over the city. Big Brothers Big Sisters approved me to become an individual mentor. The National Council of Negro Women-Chicago Central Section appointed me to the co-chair position within the Community Service and Outreach committee. This opened the door to many more network opportunities. The greatest opportunity was becoming a community volunteer with the sorority Delta Sigma Theta, Incorporated youth initiative programs (Chicago Alumnae Chapter's Dr. Betty Shabazz Delta Academy and Delta GEMS program), empowering young ladies to be successful in every area of life. These exhilarating experiences gave me exposure to amazing individuals that are taking back their communities. Black women in power! Many with their own businesses too! Now, I'm determined to move forward.

- **My parents did their best.** Those life lessons were necessary. They developed a stronger character. Parents set the bar for you to achieve a thousand times higher than they ever did. Leave your legacy. Tell your story.

- **I am not defined by my circumstances.** People mess up. Are we no different than young children learning to walk when we are in our purpose? *"Life is a succession of lessons which must be lived to be understood." Ralph Waldo Emerson*

- **Patience, Patience, Patience.** God doesn't give anything before it is time! The divine universe is aligned in perfect order. Waiting in limbo may feel counterproductive but enjoy the rest. Once the blessings are poured down, you will have no time or energy to stop. Be ready with open arms!

- **Breakdowns are preparations for breakthrough.** When you hit the bottom, there is nowhere else to go but UP! How are you to appreciate the blessings if you never experience hardships?

> • **Fear will kill you if allowed.** Do not let emotion of fear get the best of you. It can overtake your body and cause you so much stress. The uncertainty of life is inevitable. The mission is to become a woman that is the complete opposite of fear. A woman of 100 percent Faith!

When I became a Licensed Clinical Professional Counselor in June 2015, I gained professional stability with greater opportunities. If I were laid off from my job, I would be able to provide the care for others independently. Plus, working solely for someone else just wouldn't cut it anymore. Ultimately I want to have my own counseling private practice but I am still following my dream of developing my own non-profit organization.

Everything I experienced has strengthened me. I seek counsel with peer mentors. I work for a great organization and provide private contractual services for extra income and learn the ropes of private practice. I'm still an active volunteer and busy mom with my now teenage daughter. I want to make her proud so she is able to say, "My mother owns her own, gives back, and is known. Just Google her." It's exhausting but so worth it.

Renew your outlook on life! It can feel selfish at times for wanting a career and life while being a single parent. Many will make you feel like you must put your dreams on hold.

Even in joy, know that developing your craft takes sacrifice. It means late nights and early mornings. It means swallowing your pride and asking for help. There will be disappointments and frustration along the way but you will understand why some doors closed and others opened. Don't limit yourself on how things should be.

I challenge you to surround yourself with like minds. Come out of your comfort zone. Utilize your community resources to grow in success. If you are unsure where to start, volunteer. You will be surprised at the people you can meet that can help develop your brand.

Take the "Black Butterfly" challenge. Butterflies are a symbol of transition, renewal, or rebirth. It symbolizes longevity and a SHIFT in power. It is a sign of positive change in a present situation. The old YOU goes away and becomes beautiful. Your confidence will grow tremendously. Let's grow together! Let's fly!

"Your success and happiness lies in you. Resolve to keep happy, and your joy and you shall form an invincible host against difficulties."

–Helen Keller

MO POWER TO YOU

SHADONNA MCPHAUL

"Everybody is a hero to somebody."
                    –ShaDonna "Mo" Mcphaul

I'm done, Son," is a popular term used by kids today, and that's exactly how I felt in 1996 when I graduated Douglas Byrd High School on June 8th. That time from June to November seemed like an eternity in "teenage years" but I survived part-time jobs, a broken heart, and my mom and successfully made it through summer/fall until it was time for me to depart for San Antonio, Texas to join the United States Air Force. I left Fayetteville, North Carolina two days before Thanksgiving at the tender age of 18 and, aside from having my son, made the biggest life changing decision of my life.

Since making the decision to join the military, I haven't looked back or regretted one thing. I wasn't ready for college, I knew I couldn't work fast food all my life, and most importantly I knew I had to get out of my mom, Cathy's, house because I wasn't going to make it to see 19 if I didn't.

My mom and I were so much alike that we clashed over everything. I think a lot of it was the fact that I was hard-headed and I didn't think she knew what she was talking about. I was the typical teenage girl, with the typical teenage mindset. My mom worked two sometimes three jobs at a time to ensure my brother, Tez, and I were taken care of. Tez, who is nine years younger than I, was often a big part of the battles my mom and I fought. Her always being at work put a huge responsibility on me to make sure he was cared for after school, which really cramped my style. I wanted to hang with my friends, not babysit.

Looking back, caring for my little brother actually made me less selfish. The first nine years of my life, it was "ALL ABOUT ME." I'm grateful I had the opportunity to learn to care for someone beside myself. That's where I learned caring, nurturing, mothering towards the rest of society. I learned to go out of my way to help people I come in contact with.

It was at my after-school job at Hardees's on Skibo Road that I got the idea to join the Air Force. One day all of the high school seniors were standing around talking at Hardee's about all we were going to do after graduation, when my good friend, Natasha said she was joining the Air Force. I would see the Air Force recruiting in the lobby by the cafeteria at school, and they let people out of class to take the ASVAB Test (the Military Entrance Test) but all that went over my head. During those days, I just wanted to get through class, hang out with friends, and talk to boys, and not necessarily in that order. After hearing Natasha talk about her plans, and when my stepfather, Mike, added his two cents about the Air Force, I started thinking about it more and more. Lo and behold, one day I checked my mailbox and there was a postcard from one of the local recruiters, so I thought this must be a sign from God. I took the bait and went to speak to the recruiter.

My recruiter, SSgt Anita Glass, didn't have to do too much convincing, I was sold on the Air Force when I walked into her office. The only thing I had to do from that point was pass all the tests and physicals. Everyone in my family, especially my mom's oldest sister, supported my decision to join the Air Force even though they all joined the Army or married into the Army. Growing up in Fayetteville, NC, home of the 82nd Airborne, I was familiar with the army and their early morning exercise regimen. I knew I didn't want to wake up to run every morning at O'dark thirty with the Army.

After joining, I was given the Air Force Specialty Code of a 3A0X1—that's an Information Manager or "Administrative Troop" and trained at Keelser Air Force Base, Mississippi. After about four hardcore weeks of training, I was assigned to Eglin Air Force, Florida where I served from 1997 to 2003.

During my tour at Eglin, I felt like I was on top of the world. I was out of my mama's house; I had a job, a car, and eventually my own condo after living in the Air Force dorms for the mandatory three years. At that time you couldn't tell me anything. I grew up in a military family so I knew what to expect, but the Air Force exceeded my expectations.

The Air Force was known for taking care of its people and I was a living witness. The Air Force was one big family especially when you were assigned to a smaller duty location, where everyone leaned on each other for support when our biological families were not around.

From day one, I knew I wanted to serve 20 years and that's still my plan. My time in Florida was some of the best years of my life where I made some lifelong friends. During those six years, I was truly molded into the woman I am today. During "my former life" as I so often refer to my earlier years, I believe I was no different from the average young woman trying to make sense of the world and my new life as a member of the United States Air Force. I made the same mistakes as a lot of other young adults. Today, I like to think of myself as being more mature and grounded. I still make mistakes, but I recover from them easier and a lot faster.

When I received my first credit card and bought my first condo in Shalimar, Florida I felt like I was living the life. I went out almost every weekend with my girls, "Eglin's Finest," and even had a license plate on the front of my 1998 Chevy Metro that said so. "Eglin's Finest" were a bunch of 20 year old females who all worked part-time jobs to supplement our military income to keep our grooming up. We always had our hair and nails done, and wore a new outfit when we stepped on the scene. That was around the time "Destiny's Child" was huge. We frequented the "King of Clubs" to sing Karaoke every Thursday Night and performed "No, No, No Part 2." Those were the days. Although I missed my friends at Eglin, I've never had a problem making new friends and bonding with other women at my other assignments. I'm one of the lucky ones. Many get kicked out for various reasons, but I had the honor of being able to serve my country. Moving every couple of years is a part of military life that everyone gets used to, but no one really likes.

From Eglin, I had many more exciting assignments: Kunsan AB, Korea; Pope Air Force Base, North Carolina; Osan AB Korea; Ramstein Air Base Germany; and temporary duties to Keesler Air Force Base, Mississippi; and deployments to Kuwait, the United Arab Emirates and Afghanistan and Joint Base Pearl Harbor Hickam. It was there when I had my "Ah Ha" moment to start Mo's Heroes.

In November 2011, I had the opportunity to volunteer at the "Hiring our Heroes" Job Fair where First Lady Michelle Obama was the guest speaker. During that time I wondered if our homeless veterans had decent clothes and were properly groomed; could they get a job and ultimately not be homeless anymore?

I didn't think about it for a couple of years and I went on enjoying my life, partying with my friends. I was single with no kids, had just purchased my first home, and was foot-loose and worry free. Although I heard Mrs. Obama's message about hiring Veterans, I felt the fact that I had been in the Air Force since I was 18 years old made wanting to care for our Veterans a natural longing. Being in the military had been my job and I loved every minute of it.

Volunteering was a part of my daily life since I was a child. That's how I get my blessing. I tell people, "It's totally free to care." Even as a child, I remember going door-to-door when it was time to do school fundraisers. When I was in the second grade, I raised over $500 for the March of Dimes. I didn't know I was volunteering, I just knew I wanted my class to win a Pizza party and I wanted to win a prize.

In May 2013, I revisited my idea to help homeless Veterans get back on their feet and Mo's Heroes was born. It was exactly six months after I gave birth to my first and only son, Charles. I'm now 35-years-old, a single woman in the Air Force, raising a son and starting a 501(c)3 nonprofit.

If you are interested in starting a 501(c)3 here are some steps to follow:

- Determine the type of non-profit you want to start.
- Choose a name.
- Apply for the name with your state. (Check with the state to make sure the name is available. If so, the name can be reserved for a small fee.)
- Prepare a mission statement (make it as compelling as possible in one or two sentences).
- Talk to an attorney with experience in nonprofits about Bylaws and Articles of Incorporation.
- File the Articles of Incorporation.
- Apply for the employer identification number.
- Establish a relationship with an accountant by either hiring one or finding one willing to barter or work pro bono.
- Open a bank account.
- Apply for tax exempt status (Federal, State, local). Federal applications must be filed within 27 months of the organization's establishment date.
- Draft By-laws.
- Form a Board of Directors.
- Contact the state's Department of Commerce or Attorney General's office for fundraising guidelines.
- Apply for non-profit mailing permit, if bulk mailing will be utilized.
- Design a logo.
- Secure a domain name and design web site.
- Establish social media accounts (Facebook, Twitter, Google Plus, etc.).

These are the basic beginning steps. You will also need to make a budget, a plan for record keeping and accounting system, among other things. I have to thank my stepmother, Sandra, who is an accountant for helping me with this checklist.

I followed all those steps. The mental stress of being a new single mom never stopped me. The financial stress of being a new single mom with a new business never stopped me. The physical stress of being a new single mom in the military never stopped me, and neither did the naysayers and haters.

The whole time I was going through the process of starting Mo's Heroes my faith in my God never wavered, even on my toughest days and hearing "NO" almost every day. "We can't help you right now," was a constant response I received. I knew that I had to keep going because there were men and women who sacrificed everything to serve our country and they didn't have anything to show for it but memories. Some of the memories may be good and some not so good. I once volunteered at a homeless shelter and met a lady with a son around the same age as my son and that's when I became motivated to make a change. Not only did I have to worry about me, now I had a son to think about, and fear of becoming a "Homeless Veteran," I began to Shift. Almost everything about my life changed. I no longer wanted to party and hang out. All I wanted to do was work. The idea of not being able to take care of my son scared the living daylights out of me and I knew I had to make some major moves. I had always been creative when it came to making money. I remember as a kid selling homemade "Icee". My wheels started turning. Shaved Ice/Snow Cone business is huge in Hawaii. I wanted to bring a little bit of Hawaii back to North Carolina. I started laying the foundation for not only Mo's Heroes, but Mo Snow, LLC, a business that I run my with mother and brother.

I also have a major passion for event planning and coordinating events, so I started Memories with Mo Event and Party Planning Services. I planned my first birthday party at the tender age of five and haven't stopped since. My whole military career I was always the first one to volunteer to plan the Squadron Holiday Parties or anything that was going to be a good time. I even gave myself the fictitious title of "Non-Commissioned Officer In Charge (NCOIC), of Morale and Good Times."

As everything started coming together I was being blessed with small victories that motivated me more and more each day. It even got to the point I had to make a heart breaking decision to let my son live with my mom for a year. It was difficult for me but she was overcome with joy. See Charles is her only grandchild and she "harassed" me for years to give her one. I battled with the decision but at the end of the day, I knew that was the best decision for all of us. By now I was at the 17-year point in my Air Force Career, I didn't have a Family Care Plan, and I needed to get myself in a position to have a smooth transition out of the military. The fact that I had such a supportive family, especially my mom, is the BIGGEST reason I was able to share this story today. If it had not been for them putting my mind at ease that my son was being taken care of, I would not have been able to concentrate on starting Mo's Heroes, Mo Snow, Memories with Mo Event and Party Planning Services, and all other opportunities that I was blessed enough to say "YES" to.

My mom and I have always had a great relationship, even during my wild and crazy teenage years when she threatened to send me to reform school almost every day. She taught me so much by being independent, hardworking, and to always have my own, and to be responsible for those I brought into this world. She had always had my back from day one no matter what it was that I wanted to do. From cheerleading, track, driver's education, joining the military, starting Mo's Heroes, and helping me with Charles. Her dedication to my military career was key to me being who I am. Even as I write this story she is watching Charles. I can't even put into words what a huge part she played in my life especially now as I'm so busy organizing Mo's Heroes. She knows what it means to me to be able to help Veterans reach their fullest potential and how that passion motivates me to be the best mom I can be to Charles.

As each day passes my brothers and sisters in arms fully embrace the work I'm doing with Mo's Heroes. It's because of the relationships I made over the years that I am so passionate about getting Mo's Heroes off the ground.

Many returning veterans are caught in a normally inescapable conundrum. They need to work to make the life changes that can lead to economic self-sufficiency and greater personal opportunity, but are unable to access meaningful work due to lack of experience, skills, and the support required to successfully enter the civilian labor market.

As a result, many of the returning veterans are inextricably caught in a vortex of false starts. They soon fall further and further behind, and eventually become resigned to a dependency on government support. Many veterans need to be aggressively encouraged and engaged with high levels of accountability.

Nothing can describe the feeling I get when one of the veterans I work with calls, emails, or texts me good news about their life and how things are changing for the better. I remember getting a text message from one of the Veterans I served telling me she was offered a job from Veterans Affairs. We were both excited and could not believe that everything was falling into place for her.

I always try to remind them that I walked in their shoes and experience a lot of the same disappointments that life dealt all of us but NEVER to give up. The roads are going to be tough, the nights are going to be cold and lonely sometimes but if you just have Faith that God is doing something to change our situations, our situations will get better.

We all sacrificed so much. Birthdays, anniversaries, graduations, first days of school, last days or school, you name it and we missed it because of the promise we made to our Country to protect and defend it. It would break my heart into a million pieces if one of my war buddies ended up homeless or living in a shelter when I know there are resources to help them. If I had my way, I would personally give any Veteran in need a financial helping hand but, I believe using the knowledge and resources that I have acquired through my years of military service will be more beneficial than me just giving someone money, which I've done several times in the past. There were times I needed a helping hand and those same war buddies are there for me as I'm preparing to retire from the Air Force in November 2016.

If you or anyone you know find themselves in a situation where they just don't know where to turn, please reach out to Mo's Heroes or another agency because help is available. We can be reached at www.mosheroes.org or by calling 1-844-Mos-Hero.

Here are some tips I would recommend to a Veteran or a family member of a Veteran to take to start the process to get where they want to be:

1. Register at your local Veteran Affairs Office. To find the nearest one visit www.va.gov. If you are not satisfied with the service you receive there, don't give up. There are others.

2. Keep records and document everything. If it's not in writing, it didn't happen.

3. Find a Support Group to help you deal with the issues you and your family member(s) are facing. A lot of members of the military face the same barriers and you do not have to walk the road alone.

4. If you are not ready for a support group, please find someone you trust or can depend on to help you start the process. The hardest part of anything is getting started.

5. Keep an open mind. There are a lot of benefits and opportunities that you and/or your family member(s) are entitled to and can take advantage of because of the time the Veteran served in the military.

6. Put your pride aside and ask for help. I know first-hand how hard that can be, but please don't suffer in silence.

7. Make a list of things you want help achieving. Where you may be weak, someone is strong.

8. Don't prejudge or assume everyone is out to get you or "This will not work". Everyone deserves a fair chance to prove who they are. Don't let past wrong doings keep you from future blessings.

9. Pray, Pray, and never lose hope.

STANDING ON GOD'S PROMISES

BY LORA SPENCER, J.D., M.B.A.

"For I know the plans I have for you… plans to prosper you… plans to give you hope and a future."

–Jeremiah 29:11 (NIV).

Nothing is a surprise to God. For these are the scriptures upon which I rely, repeat, and recite with every being of my soul when I'm experiencing a *Shift*. I am not everything you see—I'm not who you think I am—I'm far from perfect. I've been psychologically battered, bruised, and battled-tested. *But for God*, I've overcome, I've won, and I continue to rise. I stand on his promises.

Regardless of where you are in life, where you started, or where you stalled, I hope to inspire you to never give up, pursue your hopes, and capture your dreams. I offer you five tenets to living and enjoying the life God promised you. But you must be open, you must be ready, you must be committed to *Shift*, and you must stand on his promises.

"Out of the huts of history's shame. I rise. Up from a past that's rooted in pain."

–Mayo Angelo

Accept and Embrace Who You Are

Often the lack of acceptance of who you are is rooted in the past and based upon your experiences.

My past struggles with acceptance are seeded in my child-hood. My mother and father married at the age of sixteen and eighteen, respectively. Neither of my parents graduated from high school, although my dad eventually earned his GED. My parents were factory workers, and my dad, being the hard-working master craftsman, built our modest three-bedroom brick home with his bare hands to care for his family. Despite all outward appearances, and my parents' best efforts, they struggled to make ends meet. One of my worst childhood memories is when the hardware store repossessed my bright red shiny bicycle. I remember seeing a man parked at the end of our driveway. The man got out of his car and snatched my bicycle. I ran into the house and screamed, "A man stole my bike!" My mother never revealed that my bicycle wasn't stolen. Instead she tried to hide the fact that my bicycle had been repossessed—they just couldn't make the payments. That night, I cried myself to sleep, thinking, *If only I had not left my bike in the front yard and so close to the road.*

My parents divorced after 14 years, 1 month, and 10 days of marriage. I was 12 years old. My mother then became a 30-year-old divorcée with four children. She would soon have five. She was an excellent seamstress and to make ends meet, she sewed our clothes. I remember my mother unable to afford to buy me jeans like other children. The uniform of choice, day in and day out consisted of gray polyester slacks, a white or light blue thin cotton blouse, and denim wedge heel sandals with yellow daisies. Even in the early winter, this was the uniform. Oh, and I had one coat that I wore to school, church, and out to play. In my house, all-purpose truly meant all-purpose. When I didn't wear slacks, I wore home-sewn (not tailored) or hand-me-down polyester dresses and skirts. During the 1980's it was all about Nike, Levi, and Izod. To a young girl with little means, it seemed as if everyone except me wore one or more of these brands, and everyone carried a backpack with the highly visible Nike swoosh. I carried a home-sewn satchel.

I considered school to be torture. Children teased me about the clothes I wore, my wavy hair, and my height. I later recognized the beauty and value of having naturally long beautiful hair and long legs. Although being tall also meant having large feet.

One early winter I stood at the bus stop in my denim daisy sandals—with my toes curled and nearly frozen, trying to keep my feet warm. I looked at all the other little girls' shoes. They had on warm, pretty boots. Although I longed for boots of my own, I said, "I like your shoes." They laughed and shouted, "We don't like your shoes!" I was so hurt.

My mother did her best to put clothes on our backs and food on the table, and my siblings and I did our part. During the scorching summer months I worked in the tobacco fields pulling and chopping weeds. During the winter, I spent my weekends bundling tobacco leaves in a cold barn and/or chopping and stacking wood to burn in our wood stove. This saved on the electric bill. And when my mother purchased a box of cereal and the box contained eight servings, we stretched it to eight or more servings by measuring our cereal in a measuring cup. When we didn't have milk, we used water. We also became master gourmet sandwich makers—my favorite was mayo and tomato on bread.

As a pre-teen, I hated my life. My parents were divorced, the kids at school were unbearable, and as my mother would say, we were "broke." I felt alone, anxious, and angry and I wanted it all to end. I couldn't see past that moment in time. Seeking a way out, one day I stood in the kitchen looking out of the window thinking that to live I must die. I opened the kitchen drawer and retrieved a bottle of aspirin. Trembling, I poured the tablets in my hand and I started to cry. My chest hurt. I wanted to swallow the pills, but I couldn't. I didn't really want to die. I was just a 12 year-old hormonal kid going through an emotional storm.

Overcome with anxiety, I ran as fast as I could to a gigantic beautiful oak with an enormous trunk, sturdy branches, and lavish green leaves that we called The Big Tree. Neighborhood kids gathered at The Big Tree to play, race, and fight. In fact, that's where I met the neighborhood girls who picked on me. And where I delivered The Big Tree beat down.

When I arrived at The Big Tree, I cried harder and louder. I sobbed so much that I almost had an anxiety attack. My heart raced, my hands and face were sticky with perspiration, and my chest felt like it would explode. I wailed, and then I prayed. I challenged God: "Why was I born? What is Your plan for me? Did I have purpose?" Then suddenly, as I sat with my eyes tightly closed, I felt a light breeze upon my face, and I heard a soft whisper. God spoke to me. He said, "Don't worry, My child. You will have trials and tribulations, but when you turn 30, I will surely bless you."

Let Go of Anxiety

In large part, I lived an anxious life. Anxious about my future based on my past. Anxiety led me to seek constant control over every facet of my life because I dared to depend on others. Anxiety is a thief—robbing you of life. If you are living your life with anxiety, I challenge you to let go, trust God, and stand on His promises.

Anxious About the Future

When I was a little girl I never went to bed without eating, but the truth is our food was rationed. My mother repeatedly shouted, "Get out of that kitchen, that food must last the rest of the month." In fact, we had to ask permission to open the refrigerator door. To deter us from sneaking food, my mother drew measurements on the containers. When I pilfered food, I tried to mask the container so my mother wouldn't notice.

The anxiety I experienced as a child about what I was going to eat or wear only increased as I grew older. I knew one day I would be responsible for providing for myself. What was I going to do? I never wanted to be hungry; I wanted to eat what I wanted to eat, when I wanted to eat. I never wanted to be without clothes; I never wanted to have just one coat; I never wanted to be cold; I never wanted to wear sandals in the winter, and I never wanted to work in a tobacco field again.

I look back and think about all the time I spent being anxious. What did I gain? Nothing. What did I lose? I lost peace of mind. Anxiety attacks the mind. Even with my mother's limited income I never went hungry or shirtless. Even as a young adult starting out in life, trying to find my way, I never went hungry or shirtless. I wish the universe would refund all the time I spent being anxious about what God had already provided. Do not let anxiety rob you of life.

Don't Be Afraid to Start Over

As a 5'10" inch high school freshman, I caught the attention of the local girls basketball coach. He asked if I would try out for the girls' basketball team. I said yes and I promised to meet him in the gym after school. He was elated, but there was one problem—I had no intention of trying out for the team.

I knew if I asked my mother if I could play basketball the answer would be the same answer I received when I asked if I could be a Girl Scout, a Brownie, and a member of the 4-H Club. She always gave a resounding, "NO—I DON'T HAVE ANY MONEY FOR THAT!" This was my mother's standard response.

I avoided Coach, and every afternoon after school I sprinted to the bus. After a week of playing cat and mouse, he stood waiting at my bus and said, "Spencer, I thought you were coming to the gym." Cornered and emotionally exhausted, I confessed, "I'm not coming. I can't play basketball. I don't know how to play. I've never played, and we're poor. My mother doesn't own a car, and she don't have any money for shoes or after game meals." Without hesitation he asked, "What do you want to be when you grow up?" I had a Perry Mason moment.

Perry Mason was a famed television criminal defense attorney that originally aired between 1957-1966. I watched the reruns in the 1980's. Every episode he was dressed in a black or gray suit, crisp white shirt, and a black sleek tie, and every episode he won his case. I loved Perry Mason, and as a pre-teen girl, I pretended I was Perri Mason. Perry didn't wear Nike, Levi, or Izod, nor did he carry a swoosh backpack—he carried a briefcase. And as Perri Mason, I held my head high, lifted my chin, erected my chest, and confidently strutted into elementary school. In my mind, I wasn't going to school. Dressed in my gray polyester slacks, and carrying my "briefcase," I was going to court. That's how I made it through the pain of elementary and junior high school. I played a game, and the game was seeing myself as Perri Mason going to court every day as an intelligent, successful, well dressed attorney.

With that I answered, "A lawyer." He then asked, "How are you going to pay for college?" I was puzzled because I had never heard of college. I didn't know what college was, but I immediately discerned that it must be a form of higher education and a necessary requirement for becoming a lawyer. Naive, I said, "Lawyers have to go to college?" My parents didn't know about college, they knew about hard work. The majority of the residents in my small Kentucky town were farmers, factory workers, or unemployed.

I will never forget the compassion in Coach's eyes as he vowed to buy my shoes, provide my meals, and furnish my transportation. He then said, "If you work hard, I promise I will get you to college on a girls basketball scholarship so you can become a lawyer." I was surprised. Not only did I not know anything about college I didn't know girls played basketball in college. I didn't have a clue.

Coach kept his word. He purchased my shoes, fed me after the games, and provided transportation. When he couldn't drive me personally, he arranged for a teammate's family to pick me up or take me home. I, too, kept my word. I worked hard, played three and a half years of high school basketball, and by my senior year I earned multiple-year All District—Region and State—honors. I was named to various tournament teams, secured berths on several All-Star teams, received USA Today Girls Basketball All-American honorable mention, and I was offered 20 Division I girls college basketball scholarships. Basketball would be my way out. In four years, I would become a first generation college graduate, so I thought. Instead, I went through a devastating *Shift.*

My mother experienced a heart attack at age 28, a second one at age 32, and a third at age 36. Ultimately, at the tender age of 39, God called my mother home. Her weary and failing heart would beat no more. My mother ran a good race, she fought a great fight, she did the best she could, the best she knew how, with the best she had. I left college immediately following her death. During the next few years I felt lost and confused—questioning the next steps in my life, *anxious* and *worrying* about my future and if my life was over.

Let Go of Worry

Worrying – It won't work out.

Let me first say, things always work out. They may not work out the way you planned, but they always work out. And most often, better than you planned yourself. Whatever your past, whatever your present, you can trust that your future is in God's hands.

I spent my early twenties adjusting to my reality that I would not become a lawyer. I worked as a pharmaceutical technician, customer service representative, and a licensed realtor. Then I experienced a climactic career shift. At age 30, God fulfilled his Big Tree promise. He blessed me to join the then number one pharmaceutical company in the world. When I applied, they were undergoing an expansion. The expansion allowed for an additional 538 new positions and the company received over 45 thousand résumés. I obtained one of the 538 positions. I share this not to boast but to give God the glory and to illustrate the magnitude and magnificence of his blessings, and the fulfillment of his promises. Whatever your past, whatever your present, you can trust that your future is in God's hands. Just stand on his promises.

At this company I experienced stellar successes. Yet, after nine years, I lost my job—I was downsized. When I received the call, I heard the "Unfortunately… blah, blah, blah" script. However, my ears went numb to the words spoken. I raised my right hand to the heavens and mouthed, "Thank you, Jesus." At the time, I didn't completely understand what was happening but I knew I had to continue to stand on his promises, and embrace the *Shift*.

God was *shifting* me into my destiny, *shifting* me to complete the good work he started in me, *shifting* me to reap the seeds planted within my spirit so many years ago, and *shifting* me towards His greatest blessing—a blessing I never predicted.

Have your plans been derailed? Have you felt lost, confused, or stuck? Listen, your life is NOT over. Nothing is a surprise to God! I challenge you to recognize and believe that God has a plan for you. He sees the end from the beginning. Embrace the *Shift*. God is making you anew. Do not be afraid to start again, start over, or simply just start.

I *started again* when I returned to college, I *started over* after ending my twelve year career at two biopharmaceutical companies, and I simply *started* my professional degree programs later than I envisioned in life. Despite holding my college education in abeyance for 2 ½ years, and forgoing a full four-year athletic scholarship, God more than provided. I eventually earned my Bachelor's Degree, a Master of Business Education, and a Juris Doctor. Won't He do it!

Be Open to Give and Receive Unconditional Love

My first love was my father. I loved him so much; I wanted so badly to be like him. I'm embarrassed to say, but when I learned that boys stood up to use the bathroom, I tried standing to use the bathroom too because I knew that's how my dad used the bathroom. However, I quickly aborted this operation.

When my parents were married I followed my dad around everywhere. I wanted to be wherever he was, doing whatever he was doing. Whether that meant cutting the grass, painting a fence, or working under the hood of a dilapidated car. I was just happy being with him—a true daddy's girl. When my parents divorced I spent less time with him. I guess that's par for the course of being a product of a broken home.

While I consider my dad my first true love, my grandmother taught me unconditional love. Anyone who knows me knows I live and breathe for my grandmother. She taught me unconditional love and deposited the love of God in me, and a spirit of belief and faith that God is always in control.

As a child, I wanted to spend every weekend with my grandmother. When I asked to come over, she always said, "Yes," unless she was working one of her three jobs, as a restaurant manager, a country club kitchen manager, or a home healthcare aide. When I didn't spend Saturday night with her, she picked me up on Sundays for church. It seems like yesterday she was giving me two quarters to put in Sunday school, and a dollar to put on the church table. Sunday afternoons were filled with love and a variety of foods, like fried chicken, country ham, turkey, greens, macaroni and cheese, sweet potatoes, lima beans, potato salad, green beans, black eye peas, cornbread, pecan pie, rum cake, and sweet tea, just to name a *few*. No special occasion—it was just Sundays at grandmothers— filled with love.

Eventually, I spent more time at my grandmother's house, and ultimately my senior year I moved into her home. Every weekday morning, Grandmother rose early to cook my breakfast while I slept. I awoke to the smell of homemade biscuits and gravy, country ham, eggs, and grits. Other mornings I ate hot biscuits with her homemade strawberry jam. I ate while she ironed my clothes and made my bed. Similarly, every night she prepared a hot meal. My favorites were her homemade salmon patties and fried potatoes, and her fabulous meatloaf served with green beans and mashed potatoes. Life was so pleasant, so different from the life I lived with my mother.

Although I found and experienced unconditional love with my grandmother, I still held to the covenant I made to myself when I was 12-years-old—I would never marry nor have children. I wanted to become a lawyer, travel the world, and make up for all my lost summers as a child. I saw marriage as a curse and I wanted to depend on no one but myself. Also, I feared being financially responsible for a child. My childhood left me scarred and spoiled to the thought of marriage and children. Until…

It was three days before I started law school when I met him. He was everything I didn't know I wanted and needed. When we met I wasn't ready to give or receive unconditional love. Have you ever been in that place in your life when you met someone that you were not ready to receive? Well, that was me. BUT, praise God, he was ready for me. So much so that he waited and waited and waited. When God brings you the person of whom your rib belongs, you can't run him away. Lord knows I tried.

Although I dated, I still reminded myself of the promise not to marry. But then, one day about eight months before I met him I had a change of heart. I was a leader in my career, a leader in my household of one, a leader in my family, and I grew weary of being the leader. For once, I wanted someone to lead me. All of a sudden, all the success in the world meant nothing without having someone special to share my life. I turned to God and I took out a piece of paper and wrote out the characteristics I desired in my husband. I wrote 21 things on my list and I prayed over the list with scripture and placed it in my faith box. I was careful to tell God that my list represented the minimum of what I wanted. For I was reminded of God's word, "…the mind cannot conceive… the blessings I have for you," and I didn't want to block or minimize my blessing.

From day one, he gave me 110%. Yet, I wrestled with destiny like Jacob wrestled with God. And just like Jacob, I lost, yet God blessed me anyway. After years of wrestling with God about him, I decided to look at my list. Of the 21 things on my list, he had 19, and those 19 he had from day one. I just didn't realize it. Love wasn't hiding in plain sight; I just wasn't looking. Despite living more than a thousand miles apart, and my life *shifting* into a new direction—attending law school while working full time, and driving three hours round trip four days a week to study law, and him relocating from one part of the country to another—juggling his career as a physician/lawyer, we made it work.

As I checked off the 20th item on my list, God revealed to me another list. God not only granted me what I wanted, he blessed me with someone with qualities I didn't know I needed. Seven is the number of completeness and perfection. And seven years to the date of what represents our eternal beginning, God completed the work he started in us—we were married.

I share my story of unconditional love because when it is the unconditional love of my grandmother and my husband that I realized what matters most. Whatever you are going through, I implore you to open yourself up to giving and receiving unconditional love. You cannot expect God to bless you and release you from your emotional prison if you continue to hold yourself in bondage.

Ask God to remove anything in your heart that is preventing you from giving and receiving unconditional love. In the meantime, wait, trust, and believe He will give you the desires of your heart.

I leave you as I greeted you. God knows you, He knew you before you were formed in your mother's womb. He knows the plans He has for you, plans for your future, plans to prosper you. You are right where He knew you would be, in this time, place, and space. Stop giving the devil power by saying, "The devil's always busy." Instead, I challenge you to give God the credit and the glory. Stand on God's promises and declare victory because He's *shifting* you into your breakthrough. God is pushing you out of your nest, not so you can fly, but, so you can soar!

5 Tenets to Living and Enjoying the Life God Promised You

1. Accept and embrace who you are—God knew you before he formed you in your mother's womb (Jeremiah 1:15 (NIV).

2. Don't be anxious.

3. Don't be afraid to start over.

4. Don't worry.

5. Be open to give and receive unconditional love.

THE ROAD LESS TRAVELED

BY TOMAYIA COLVIN

"Two roads diverged in a wood, and I—I took the one less traveled by. And that has made all the difference."
                                                                    –Robert Frost

The school bell rang. It was August 25, 2014 and the first day of my dream job. The job that I'd wanted for a long time. I started the day as a Photography, Journalism, and Yearbook teacher at a new school and district. The students were as excited as I was. We were going to learn about photography and creating the school yearbook. *What could be better than that?* I thought.

Slowly we got into our groove and created layouts and individual projects and I was teaching my passion. There were a few hiccups along the way but nothing too significant. When winter came and with the new year, we were told we would be getting a new principal. If you know anything about education, you know that the principal sets the tone for the building. Suddenly the demands changed, and expectations were set higher. More paperwork was being required as the new regime worked to turn the school around.

Regardless of how many classes and preps you had, the paperwork and demands increased and slowly my love of teaching started to leave. I was going to work and things were getting out of control.

As a result, I was depressed. I found myself having anxiety attacks and migraines every morning when it was time to go to school. The thought of the cumbersome paperwork, the dreaded walkthroughs to evaluate my teaching, and stories of the violence going on inside the building were all taking its toll. Finally, reality set in; it was time to leave my dream job. Thoughts filled my mind: *How can you leave a career that you love? What about the students?*

I had wanted to become a high school teacher and change the lives of my students. I wanted to give them a quality education that so many of my friends missed out on. I grew up in a small, urban neighborhood in Houston surrounded by my family.

To my family, especially my father, education was paramount. I knew I wanted to go to college because it would be my exit out of the neighborhood. I was a pretty good student in high school, making mostly As and Bs and never got into too much trouble.

While in high school I had two teachers who were influential and the reason I became a teacher. Ms. Lindsey and Ms. Deese had strong impacts on my life, and I wanted to be like them and truly make a difference in the lives of children. They were very supportive and encouraging me to pursue my aspirations. They often told me how awesome I was, and even appointed me to leadership roles in the school. That was a challenge, but it helped me learn how to be a leader and role model to my classmates.

College was a rocky and trying experience. When I enrolled, I had to take a placement test. I scored below average and was placed in remedial classes. I was surprised to find out I was not prepared for college academically. The high school I graduated from was one of the lowest ranked in the state, and I had to take remedial math and English courses just to get on an equal playing field with the other students. There were times I was placed on academic probation and was actually suspended from the university. I had to take classes at a community college, and at that time I was diagnosed with Major Depressive Disorder. I didn't know what was causing me to sleep so much and to not have the desire to complete my assignments.

After being diagnosed with major depression, and after getting proper help, I was able to enroll back into the university. I was able to focus during this second chance at completing my degree program. When I found out I was pregnant with my daughter, I knew I had to graduate college. I had to be someone because I was going to have a little person depending on me. I ended up making the Dean's list and received academic scholarships and the opportunity to study abroad in Paris, France. All because I was given the proper help from the university and the support that I needed. This taught me that even though we can't control where we come from, we can take the steps to improve our circumstances.

One of my most rewarding moments was when I assisted 25 students in filling out their college applications and financial aid paperwork. This gave them the opportunity to further their education and to really make a difference in the world. They were appreciative beyond my wildest dreams. Many of their parents were high school graduates but had not gone any farther. They had no knowledge of the application process so I was a vital component.

One of the reasons I understood the importance of getting help throughout the application process was because I hadn't gotten the help I needed back then. I went to the college and career center at my high school but they didn't give me much assistance. I couldn't really turn to my parents or grandparents for help because even though they were very supportive, they hadn't gone to college themselves. My grandfather had a sixth-grade education and my grandmother completed a technical school and worked as a nurse's aid. So helping prepare students for college was not only fulfilling their dreams, it was fulfilling mine as well.

After graduating college, I went right into teaching and a few years later I became an entrepreneur making scrapbooks, which transitioned into me taking pictures of my friends and family. As business picked up, I felt a bit overwhelmed with the demands of teaching and running a full-time photography business during the evening.

What was becoming important to me was finding a work and life balance. I had another child and I was struggling to be both a great parent and a great teacher. When I came home from work the first thing I did was sit at the computer; sometimes I was in the same spot for hours catching up on emails and responding to clients. Some things were being left unattended and my home life was a disaster. My children were missing school project deadlines, I didn't have time or energy to buy groceries, and things were in complete disarray. I knew that I wanted to leave the classroom; I just didn't know how soon the day would come. I wasn't sure just yet if it was time for me to take the leap of faith. Becoming an entrepreneur was scary. And I was sad because I had to leave my heartbeats, my students, in the hands of another teacher. One of the most fulfilling parts of my career was having the opportunity to change lives every single day, but if I walked away from the classroom, I thought I would no longer have that same opportunity.

The day finally came and I decided that it was time for me to leave because I was tired of the mental meltdowns, anxiety attacks, and severe depression. I resigned from my teaching position unplanned so I did not have a savings account or money set aside. My family was in complete shock that I had taken this huge step, and boy was I afraid. For a few months it was challenging and being honest it still is now. No one on the outside knew how bad it was because I hid it so well. One day my daughter wanted $10 for a boogie board and I didn't have it. That was probably one of my lowest moments financially, next to almost being evicted from my apartment. The clients weren't coming in like I'd hoped, and photography can be very seasonal so I was having a hard time making ends meet. I remember thinking that we are going to get evicted, and I am going to have to tell people that I made this huge mistake about quitting my job and being a full-time photographer. If it were not for my photographer friends, I would have indeed been homeless. It was at that moment that I had to rely fully on God and the support system He had put in my life. For this to work and for me to be successful, I knew I was going to have to put my everything into my career. So at that moment I was on the brink of losing it all, I still had to push myself forward.

For anyone thinking of starting their own businesses or shifting into a different career or season, I strongly suggest you have a relationship with God. I would also encourage you to be authentic and honest with yourself about the situation that you are facing. Accept the fact that entrepreneurship is a journey, and this is the journey you chose.

Having a support system is also very important. There are going to be some extremely rough times ahead, and you must have someone that you can share your inner thoughts with.

Here are some specific things you can do to make ends meet as you pursue your passion:

1. Set a monthly budget and work from an envelope system. Use a cash only way of paying bills by designating an envelope for each of your spending categories. When the envelope is empty you can't borrow from other envelopes.

2. Limit discretionary spending. Cut back as much of the fat as you can, which may mean not eating out or limiting your coffee stops each week.

3. To make the ends meet until you're financially stable, take on a part-time job if necessary.

In order for your passion to become a successful career, building a brand is essential. Building a brand from the ground up is an ever-changing process and should be a living document, so if something isn't working and you need to change it, you can. I've built the brand of my photography business on one key value: Trust. My clients trust that I will provide a quality product, take amazing photographs, and deliver.

The journey from going to a steady paycheck to becoming an entrepreneur is not an easy one. If it were easy, then everyone would be doing it. But it definitely has its rewards. I get to work from home and get my kids off to school every day. I also have the freedom to make my schedule, but at the same time I depend on my clients for my income.

When I started my business, it was important for me to build my brand, so I attended lots of networking events in Houston. There were times where I bartered my services with other business, because like me, they didn't have enough money to pay either. I photographed a lot of sponsored events and waived my fee to have the recognition and build my brand awareness; partnering and building relationships in the process. Not all of them were good, but most worked out and those relationship are still strong. If you are starting your career from the ground up, trust the process and be willing to do the work necessary to build.

Whatever moment you are in as an entrepreneur or if you are still working a corporate job, that is your moment and you have to live it. When I wake up, I don't know if I'm going to get a client that day, or if I'm going to have an unhappy customer, or if the decision that I made yesterday is going to impact positively on my business this week. I make every effort and I live in the moment.

Right now what is pushing me forward on this journey is that even though I'm not in the classroom, I still get to impact students. As a photographer I take senior pictures of high school students. On every single session I get to pour into the life of a teen. During these times I've found ways to mentor them in different ways. I help them with their college applications, provide resources to help them decide on a career path, and offer them support they may not be getting at home.

Through photographing them, with every click, I let them know they are important and try my best to boost their self esteem. I applaud them and celebrate their academic, athletic, and extra-curricular successes in school by attending awards ceremonies and games when my schedule permits. It's one of the things I miss about being in the classroom. One of the most rewarding experiences as a teacher was watching a student get it, who never really understood a specific concept before. Or they finally understand a text, the characters, and are able to understand a passage in a book.

If you are living your destiny, at the end of the day you sleep peacefully knowing that you're doing the right thing. God is going to see you through whatever situation that you are facing regardless of what it is.

When I set out to be a teacher, I had no idea that it didn't have to be in a traditional way.

You may be on a job or in a career where you think you aren't able to use your gifts, but guess what, there's always a way if your passion is strong and your heart is sincere. Taking the road less traveled for me has made all the difference. I didn't want to take the easy way and continue to work in a capacity that was unful-filling. I chose to be creative with my gifts. I chose to leave the classroom to pursue my dreams and purpose, and in doing so, I am still able to reach the lives that I intended. I'm still able to serve, and teach, and share, and provide support and resources to students. I had many challenges that could have turned me around but I kept my eyes on the prize and you can too.

I recently launched a photography exhibit called The Unboxed Project that showcases past teen and adult clients who display characteristics that make them stand out from the rest. It's a rare chance to celebrate those amazing teens who aren't following the pack and aren't afraid to step outside of society's box to do what they believe. I want to show them they don't have to be a particular size or do negative things like drink or do drugs to be popular.

I want to show them and you that you can be successful fol-lowing the road less traveled *too*.

THERE'S LIFE IN THE GRAVEYARD

BY SHERYL L. ENGLISH

"With everything that has happened to you, you can either feel sorry for yourself or treat what has happened as a gift. Everything is either an opportunity to grow or an obstacle to keep you from growing. You get to choose."

–Dr. Wayne Dyer

The graveyard is where we bury dead things and dead people. But let's examine ourselves for a minute; let's see what dead things we are still holding on to in our lives that keep us bound, depressed, oppressed, confused, angry, and bitter. There was a time when I was all of those things wrapped in one. I'd gone through life, event after event, tragedy after tragedy, and disappointment after disappointment without any coping mechanisms. I would wake up mad at the world—just pissed off. It took me a long time to figure out why, because to people on the outside, I was the life of the party and the perfect masquerader. You'd never know. From my earliest recollections, there was always something going on. It wasn't my fault, I just happened to be there and a part of it, willingly or unwillingly.

We lived in a well-maintained neighborhood of South Central, Los Angeles, with some of the friendliest neighbors you could ask for. I was an only child; my mother worked for Los Angeles, USC

Medical Center, often referred to as Big General. The exterior of the hospital has been used in several movies, TV shows, and even the soap opera "General Hospital." So, it sort of makes sense that my life was so filled with drama. My father was a young military police officer who made the military his career. In my younger years, he spent most of his time overseas. We didn't travel with him and I remember waiting for him to call just so I could hear his voice. When he came home on leave, I remember standing at the windows inside of the terminal at the airport waiting for his plane to land. He'd exit the plane in his uniform, standing strong and tall. He was 6'2" and seemed like a giant, but he was my daddy. He called me "Boogie." His visits were always bittersweet because as soon as I got used to him being at home, he had to leave again. I hated it, but duty called. I'd always cry when we had to take him to the airport to leave. With my daddy gone, it would be mom and me again, and some of her friends. I still tear up whenever I hear the song "Rainy Night in Georgia" by Brook Benton. When he came home, he would play it over and over. It was one of his favorites. My parents were young when they married and didn't have a good marriage. Of all the people in the world, these two really didn't know each other, which left me wondering if their only purpose for being together was to bring me into this world.

In my mother's eyes, I should have been the perfect little debutante—prim and proper and excited over pomp and circumstance. But no matter what, she always wanted me to have the best. She taught me exceptional table manners and how to speak in correct dialect. She dressed me in the best clothes and shoes, and I went to the beauty shop on the weekend. For $5.00 Miss Dorothy would press my hair. Mr. or Miss so and so is what you called grown people when I was growing up. You didn't call adults by their first name, ever. My cousin Angie and I dreaded going to the beauty shop. Miss Dorothy shampooed and pressed our hair—and burned us too. We would laugh because Miss Dorothy had big boobs and when she'd shampooed our hair, she'd darn near smother us with those things. Ah, to be young and innocent again.

By all accounts, and from the outside looking in, people assumed my life was one big fairy tale, but it was far from that. Although, I didn't have a horrible life, I definitely had experiences that in a young age other children didn't have. What I didn't realize was the good, the bad, the different definitely molded me into who I am today.

"Do you remember when he took you and wouldn't give you back to your mother? I had to go get you and he gave you to me," my aunt Doris asked one day when we were having a conversation about the past. I didn't remember that at all. I do remember other crazy things he did. He was a much older acquaintance of my mother's, and quite infatuated with her.

Once, I was in my pink pajamas; my mother, the crazy man, and I were standing in the utility room at my house. We were standing in the dark, and he was crying while my mom was talking. He turned on the gas, with the intention of killing us all. My mother grabbed me and pushed me into my room, locked the door behind us, opened the window, and out we went running down the street to a neighbor's house. They were home and took us to safety. I think the police were called because by this time, all my neighbors were out of their house. I don't even remember running and getting away from this crazy man.

There were more episodes with the crazy man. Once my mother refused to see him, he followed us on the way to the childcare center, rammed into her car, and broke her arm. One rainy night while my aunts were visiting, he shot through the living room window. We were all crawling around on the floor like we were in combat. Somehow he found my father's military address and wrote him a 45-page letter. My dad told me about it, and even though he didn't give me the details, I know it hurt him. Just the idea of another man putting us in danger and still making threats while he was away was devastating. Whatever was in that letter was cause for the FBI to sit in front of our house, day and night and follow us to school and work. So what do you do? I did like my mother does; I kept on going, like nothing ever happened. We didn't talk about it, we just went on like normal life. That's what we did. That was one of many incidents.

One afternoon, years later, my mother had a guest over who eventually stayed the night. I heard the doorbell ring and since I wasn't expecting anyone, I didn't answer it. It was a gentleman she had met at church and was a contractor who obviously came without calling, which was a no-no. Typically, if you came unannounced, we'd look through the drapes covering the window to see who it was. And sometimes the door was opened and sometimes it wasn't. I have that habit to this day. I just don't move if I'm not expecting you and neither do my children.

My mother said she didn't know why he was visiting, so she didn't let him inside because she had company. I didn't think much more of it and stayed in my room the rest of the day, until I was awakened by the loud sound of glass and screams. In a daze, I got up and here was the man from church, who seemed to be on some type of drug, jumping on my mother's guest. He was breathing like a wild animal and was strong as a bear. We were screaming trying to get him off her guest, but he wasn't budging. I didn't even think about being scared, I was just angry.

My father had a sword hanging in the hallway with some of his awards, so I grabbed it and started swinging. When that didn't work, I went for a hammer. I was beating the crap out of this man and he still wasn't fazed. Somehow, her guest got away and my mother ran to get her gun. I grabbed the gun and had every intention of putting every bullet from it in this man. She grabbed it from me, and told him if he kept coming she was going to shoot him. He kept coming like she hadn't uttered a word. My mother started shooting and he kept walking towards us so we turned and ran. Somehow, we got out the front door, and again running in our pajamas, we ran across the street to my neighbor's house. They were a nice couple that looked out for us, so we went inside and called the police.

When the police arrived and called my mother to come out, she was in shock and forgot to put the gun down. The police had their guns drawn, and I was yelling and screaming that the man was across the street in my house. When she put the gun down and a few officers came to talk to her, the rest of us went into the house with the paramedics. It took nine police and paramedics to take this man down. He was on PCP, and because he was shot they had to take him to the hospital, then jail afterwards.

We went to the police station and everyone was questioned separately. By this time, it's 5 A.M. and I was in shock and sleepy. Truthfully, I don't even remember how I got to the police station or how I got home. But when I did, it looked like hell. There was blood everywhere—on the ceiling, walls, floor. There was black latent powder all over the walls. It looked like the worst war movie everywhere. My stomach was sore from swing the hammer and I was tired from all the fighting I was doing. I told my mom that I wasn't going to work. I mean, who would. She said, yes you are. I thought she was mad, like out of her mind mad, so reluctantly I got ready for work and she dropped me off. The first thing she told me not to do was to tell my cousin Kevin. So the first thing I did was told him. In my mom's mind, what happened in our home was our business, but there was another reason too. My dad and my cousin's dad were first cousins, and if he told his dad, it would just be a matter of time before my dad would find out the whole story.

I never forgot that night, and days later I found out that the man who broke into our house died. Not from the gunshot wounds but from cardiac arrest. We never talked about it again.

From an early age I learned to be the keeper of secrets, not just mine, but other peoples' too. Some of it was shame and some of it was pride, but either way it wasn't healthy. It weighed me down and worst of all, it ruined my relationship between my dad and me. He thought I was a cohort in some of my mom's antics that I had no part in. I had seen and heard so much but I was too young to process it all, so I just buried what I had seen and heard deep inside.

My dad retired from the military and came home for good. It was an adjustment to have him there all the time. I was older now, with my own life and opinions so it was like getting to know him all over again. However, my parents' marriage was horrible. I guess it's hard to adjust to a marriage when you have been in separate places for the majority of the marriage. They just didn't get along.

After retiring, my father went to work in the Aerospace industry and told me of a clerical position for the summer. While there I met a lady named Pat, who would become a surrogate mother to me. She worked in the office where the assignments came. I would not only work for the summer but through high school and after I graduated for a total of eight years.

My parents eventually divorced and I moved out. I was working full time, taking 18 units and was stressed to the hilt from the pressures of home, so I took a break from college. The divorce was rough, but I was so glad it was over. I was always in the middle— the joys of being an only child. It was a tug a war and it was ugly. I moved back home for a while trying to figure out my next move. I had no idea what I wanted to do, but I wanted to do something. I couldn't live in my mother's house and not be employed or in school. So I had to do something quick, I did some temp work, and through a connection at church I landed a job with a management company in the entertainment industry. That also would be short lived and I was realizing that I liked being the boss more than working for the boss. But until I could figure it out, I had to have a job.

After my parents divorced, my mother retired from her job and went into real estate as her second career. She was a great salesperson and won many awards for her production and expertise. However, I thought it was crazy how driven she was to succeed and how accommodating she was to her clients. They would sometimes call at 5 A.M. Fast forward, there was an opening in the office for a receptionist and I was asked to work the position temporarily until they filled the spot. Oh course I said yes, I needed a job. I was a natural on the phone with the clients and the walk in traffic.

I went on to work with a property management company and wanted to become a property manager, which required me to obtain a real estate license. I got my license, and I went into the president's office to tell him that I'd passed the test. I was so happy that I was going to be a property manager, but that never happened. Looking back it was clearly a set up. God knew exactly what was going to happen and that real estate license just might come in handy. I would go on and do nothing with it until I got married and had my son.

That first day I picked my son up from daycare after work. I was so excited to see him, I couldn't get there fast enough. I felt guilty all day because I couldn't be with him. I just wanted to be a stay-at-home mom. Anytime that I had a bad day at work, I'd tell my then husband, "I'm going to quit my job today," and he'd say, "No, you can't do that." So I continued to work and ultimately was promoted twice. But still I just didn't want to be there. I found another brokerage that a friend of mine worked from and I joined it.

The broker taught us in a small group and I was on my way. I worked full time and did real estate part time. I remember getting my first commission check on a bank-owned property. Back then you dealt directly with the bank and you were paid the entire 6% commission. After it closed and I got my check, I looked at it and said, "I can do this." It was twice the monthly salary I was receiving on my full time job. But how was I going to do this?

I had a friend at work, she also desired to leave our company. We would go into my car at lunchtime and pray that God would bless us to have our own businesses so we could leave the company. We did this for months. *But how is this going to happen?* I thought. I was still working at the management company when I was pregnant with my daughter, and this time I had complications with my thyroid and everything was out of sorts. It didn't happen like I thought it would, but it did happen. Yes, I was terminated when I was five months pregnant and on disability. I couldn't believe it. I called a friend of mine from church named Beverley. I told her what happened and in her strong West Indian accent she said "GOOD." She had already been through a similar situation. Beverley was a single mom of five who came from Trinidad with nothing and went on to become a successful realtor. Her son wanted to become a doctor and she put him through medical school and paid for his entire education. She was a strong, confident, and a God-loving woman. She's been my closest friend ever since.

And as life would continue, there would be one more pregnancy and it was another girl. Now I had three kids all under the age of five. I was working for myself, and I didn't have to ask anyone's permission to take off and take my kids to the doctor. My marriage had its struggles but I was determined not to be divorced like my parents. I didn't want my kids to live through that. And in looking back, that is when I went from living to existing.

Moving to Texas was a no brainer. The cost of living was less then in Los Angeles and so you got a lot of bang for your buck. Besides, my mother had moved to Texas and so had my aunt Erma, my mother's younger sister, and my uncle Lonnie, her youngest brother. The majority of my mother's older siblings had always lived in Texas so it was no stranger to me at all. I loved it and I appreciated the southern hospitality right away. The people were warm and friendly and it immediately felt like home. And it didn't take me long to find work there either. I obtained my license and continued to sell real estate. I met people all over the state. And at one chance meeting, I met two ladies, Jackie and Sandy, at a PTA meeting that would change my life forever. One thing I have never been was shy about sharing my opinion, and at one PTA meeting for a new school my daughter would be attending they asked me to join the Council PTA board that would oversee the entire school district PTAs. I agreed as long as they didn't ask me to sell brownies or cookies, because I wasn't that mom. I wanted to be an advocate for the kids.

The next thing I knew, Sandy and Jackie had me running for school board trustee. I didn't have a clue, but I was a fast learner and entered the ring. I lost the election to a five-time incumbent by fifteen votes. Even though I lost, it was like I'd won. I'd go on to run two more times and didn't win. However, I stayed active in the school district, and other opportunities opened up. But things were not great at home, and I knew I had to get out of the situation. I kept thinking about my kids and didn't want them to be like me, with divorced parents so I tried to hang on. It got worse.

I'd become somewhat familiar with just moving on like nothing was happening or affecting me, but it was. It was years of issues that I never dealt with—hurts, disappointments, setbacks, etc. I'd look at people and wonder, *Why wasn't I further along? Did I miss something?* I've come to learn that God has us just where we are supposed to be. You can't look at what other people are doing, that's their journey and you have yours. I was walking around with so much dead weight, masquerading like everything was okay, because that is what I'd always done.

My world turned upside down when my mother was given six to eight months to live. I was an only child and I'd always been with her. I admired her fearlessness. To be fearless doesn't mean you are never scared. It just means you are willing to push forward in spite of your fear. My mom was a young mom determined to raise me the best she could on her own terms. She had no fear about being ill during her first battle with cancer. In fact the only time I saw fear in her eyes was when she was diagnosed with breast cancer. As crazy as her antics had been, it became clear to me she was all that I had because my dad wasn't there. As afraid as that made me feel, I put on my strong face and dealt with it. It's what I always did.

What people didn't know was that I'd been depressed as hell, and would be for some time. I was dealing with losing my mom, on top of a lot of other things from my past that I had never dealt with. Still, the days came and went and so did my mom. On a Sunday morning in 2010 she died, and I realized that she died on the 8th of August. Eight is the number of new beginnings and it was two 8's. It was a double portion of new beginnings in my life. I didn't realize until she died how much she had taught me, about life—about everything.

I know she had good intentions and meant well in her life, we all do. I truly think she was trying to find herself, because I don't think she really knew who she was. That Sunday morning, I sat at the foot of her bed until she took her last breath. And it was then that I realized that my mother died unhappy. I wasn't going to live my life that way another day. I had to leave all the dead weight in the graveyard, take my life, and live it.

Tough love is sometimes facing the truth when it doesn't feel good. I don't think my mom was happy and it feels terrible recognizing that I was headed down that same road. I can't help but wonder how different my mom would have been if there had been a Shift so she could have learned to open up and use her truth to help herself.

After some reflection I realized that for years I had just been surviving. I had put all my dreams on hold so that I could take care of everyone else. I didn't really know who the real me was. Thankfully, I began to take some difficult but necessary steps, starting with my marriage.

Four months after my mother died, I realized I had been walking around numb. I wasn't existing and I wasn't my best self, I wasn't being me at all. I couldn't live like that anymore. I had been through so much and I felt like I deserved more and better. I filed for divorce after 17 years of marriage. It was final in March 2011 and my new journey began.

I began to get to know me—the real me. I took the limits off myself, and it was an ongoing process and a great experience. I went back to school, started focusing on my business, and working on new ventures. A weight had truly been lifted. At this point I could not care less of anyone's opinion. I was working on being a better me.

Do you walk around with the deadweight of old relationships, hurts, disappointments, and setbacks? Here are some things I buried:

1. **Holding on to secrets.** I decided to look into my genealogy and I found out things about both of my parents. The truth is a beautiful thing. Along the way I discovered that my grandfather was a college professor and had a very interesting life, and an uncle was a civil rights activist. Finding out how resilient they were encouraged me to keep moving forward.

2. **Holding onto pain.** First you have to find the source. It hurt to think about some of the things I went through, and it hurt even more to blame the people I loved most in the world—my parents. My dad and I have talked through some of the issues and while there's still a ways to go, we've grown closer.

3. **Holding on to fierce independence.** I've raised my three children to work hard and be responsible young adults, but I've also raised them to trust me enough to ask for help when they need it. I watched my mom act like she could do it all by herself and she couldn't. I tried to do the same and failed as well. There's no shame in asking for help when you need it.

Dropping the dead weight has given me the motivation to go back to school, majoring in Government with an emphasis on Legal Studies at the local university. I'm involved in the community, the chamber, and I sit on several boards. More importantly, I'm still selling houses and making people's dreams come true. Being of service to others and giving back is what it is all about. There are many who are going through the same things that I have experienced. I believe everything we experience is twofold. You don't just experience it for yourself, but for others, to say to them, "Hey, if I can make it through, you can too." There are many twists and turns in life and sometimes you may get off track.

God will always send someone to give you wings to fly to the next season in your life. God knew what was in store for my life and it all happened at the appointed time so I could learn the lesson I needed at the time. And yes, sometimes you flunk kindergarten, but you don't stay in the same place forever. Be encouraged and my hope is that this gives you wings to your next season in your life. You can't run with dead weight holding on to you. So put dead things where dead things go, in the graveyard. If you leave it in the graveyard, you'll get your life back and nothing will stop you from running your race.

THE UNLIKELY ADVOCATE

BY CONTESSA LOUISE COOPER

"What I am looking for is not out there, it is in me."
                                        –Helen Keller

I never wanted to be a mother. NEVER. I was a teenager but still I felt like a messed up little girl and didn't want the responsibility for raising another person. But there I was, sitting in the doctor's office explaining that I've missed several periods. The doctor looked at my young face and back at my chart. I was 16 but I looked 13. She sighed and removed herself from the room. I knew what she was thinking because I had thought it myself. Here is another young, black girl who has ruined her life.

They left me in that sterile room to wait on the results of the pregnancy test. My slender legs swung back and forth with each second of the clock ticking. It felt like I had been in there forever when the doctor walked in and confirmed my largest fear.

I walked into the waiting room where my mother flipped through an outdated magazine. She tossed it to the side and gave me that "What's wrong with you now?" face. I lied. I couldn't tell her in front of all these people that her teenage daughter was having a baby. No, it wasn't the proper time or place. I needed to work up the courage to disappoint her, so instead I said, "I have the flu."

I told my mother my news that evening. The louder she shouted the more shame I felt. I didn't know how to respond when she asked me how this happened. The one discussion we ever had on sex was to "keep my legs closed." The screaming turned into a deafening silence as she stared at me. Finally, she looked me in my eyes and whispered, "Wait until your father gets home."

My father was the disciplinarian in our home. He was in the military and took following orders seriously, especially with his children. I fought with my father over my opinion on his harsh household rules. He was away on duty until the end of the week. My mother knew what she was doing when she said, "Wait until your father gets home" but she was really saying, "Think about what you did to yourself and this family. Now you're really going to get it." And I did.

How do you punish your 16-year-old child who's about to have a child of her own? You force her to have a child she never wanted. My parents were bible-quoting Christians and an abortion went against everything they believed in. They rejected the idea of adoption, so I believed that I had no choice but to be a mother.

A few weeks later the realization of motherhood hit me. My mother was my role model and even though I didn't agree with her methods, I respected her. She had to learn how to be a mother because her parents were not around for her. She stayed home, raised, and protected us. That was the type of parent I decided I wanted to be; one that would always be there and never give up on my child.

All of that changed. To my parents, pregnancy meant being grown and independent. I wasn't able to ask them for anything related to my baby or motherhood. If I did, their answers were sarcastic and unhelpful. I even had to find my own transportation to my prenatal appointments. I didn't want any of this.

My best friend became pregnant a few months after my announcement. Her mother was furious and put her out of the house. My parents welcomed her in with open arms and made sure that she had everything she needed. I was confused. How could they treat her better than they treated their own daughter? Was this another form of punishment?

The pregnancy was the easy part. I didn't even look pregnant. I could still fit into most of my normal clothing. No one in school knew I was expecting until I confided in a teacher that I trusted. The next day the entire school knew. It was like I was walking with a "Scarlet Letter P" around my neck. Every day I felt ridiculed for a decision that wasn't mine.

An ambulance rushed me to the hospital six weeks early. I stayed there for a week before they induced labor. They whisked him away as soon as my son was born. My recovery was slow and often painful—in and out of sleep. I didn't realize it had been a week and I hadn't seen my baby. A nurse sat me in a wheelchair and took me to the Intensive Care Nursery where he was fighting for his life. I wasn't prepared to see him in his tiny sunglasses attached to various tubes with beeping machines. She informed me that he needed a blood transfusion, had extreme jaundice, and couldn't breathe on his own.

The nurse had me change my gown, wash my arms, hands, and under my fingernails before they would let me near him. She removed him from his tiny glass box and placed him in my arms. All I could do was stare at him. He was so small, so fragile—and all mine.

"I will fight for you. I will always protect you," I whispered as I kissed him on his forehead and named him Quon.

Towards the end of the second week in the hospital, they informed me that I was strong enough to go home but Quon had to stay. It would probably be another few weeks until he would be ready to leave the Intensive Care Nursery. My mom instinct kicked in and there was no way I was going home without my baby.

I don't think I planned on not eating for three days, but I lost my appetite from the reality of my situation. I became so weak that I passed out in the nursery while visiting my son. It took all of my strength to shove him back into his plastic box before collapsing to the ground. When I opened my eyes the nurse walked over and whispered in my ear, "We won't send you home without your son. I promise."

Several weeks later I brought my tiny son home. The joyous homecoming lasted for a short time when I discovered my parents were leaving town to visit family. They were leaving me alone to care for my fragile son with his special instructions that I needed to follow to keep him healthy. When I tried to get help from Quon's father I was scolded because no boys were allowed in the house. This wasn't a boy, this was the father of my child. I recognized from that point it was Quon and me against the world.

It didn't take long for Quon to grow out of his preemie clothing into a chubby little toddler. He followed in my footsteps: loving to learn, speaking in simple sentences, and exploring his world. One day when he was three, I noticed fluid leaking from his ear and rushed him to the hospital. I was in shock. He didn't have a fever or show any other signs that he wasn't feeling well but was diagnosed with an ear infection. They kept him there for a week while they administered heavy doses of antibiotics. He was never the same after that. It was as if they switched him with another child. He wouldn't speak, respond to his name, or play with his toys. I thought he lost some of his hearing from the infection so I took him to have it checked. All of the test came back negative and his hearing was fine. We went to Children's Hospital for a full exam. I needed to know how to get my little boy back. We were there for hours while they took blood, tested his urine, and his development. We waited for the pediatrician to call us into his office. He walked into the waiting room and our eyes locked. I knew it was bad news from the expression on his face. I walked in, sat down in the leather chair, and held my breath.

The doctor's words were cold, sterile, and sent chills through my body. "Your son is mentally retarded. It will take a lot of time, resources, and money to take care of him. You are young and have your entire life ahead of you. I strongly suggest putting him in an institution where he can be well cared for. You have plenty of time to have another child if you want..."

Wait...what? I sat there for a minute while I repeated his words in my head. Did he tell me to lock away my little boy? I fought the urge to cry...to throw things...to scream. I gathered up Quon, thanked the pediatrician for his valuable opinion, and went home. It was there that I wept.

The pediatrician didn't lie. Raising Quon wasn't easy. My son communicated in grunts and cries. I didn't know when he was hungry, tired, or hurt. He would run off without me knowing and people would stare and make rude comments during some of his more extreme behaviors like falling down, banging his head on the floor, and screaming. He was also allergic to everything. None of my parenting books explained how to deal with a boy with special needs.

I hoped putting him in school would take some of the pressure off me. I would have the support of trained educators to assist me with the task of raising this child. In elementary school, they threw him in a class with children that had various levels of mental retardation. I was on bed rest and expecting my second child. I didn't have the strength to say anything about the many messy coloring pages that came in his backpack on a weekly basis. Was he learning anything in school, or was this a glorified babysitting service?

Quon and I met a pediatrician that wasn't satisfied with the previous mental retardation diagnosis and wanted to do another evaluation. She noticed Quon's lack of eye contact, severe sensitivities to light, sound and touch, hand flapping, and twirling in circles. She studied him alone. She studied our interaction together. I went over his medical history explaining his sudden change after the ear infection and heavy antibiotics. She discovered what was wrong with my baby. He was autistic.

Autism and autism spectrum disorder (ASD) is characterized by difficulties in social interaction, verbal and nonverbal communication, and repetitive behaviors. ASD can be associated with intellectual disability, difficulties with motor coordination, attention and health issues such as sleep and gastrointestinal disturbances. It was difficult finding information on autism but I read everything I could. I discovered that with proper training my son might be able to speak and learn. There were more appointments, therapists, and meetings with special educators.

It was difficult for me to keep a job. It wasn't because I was lazy or lacked skills. I was unreliable. There were various appointments marked on my calendar. I was late or had to leave early because of Quon's "meltdowns" and it was impossible for me to find after school care for him. If we were lucky he would last a week before they asked me not to bring him back. The money from public assistance and social security wasn't enough to make ends meet. I was stressed over bills daily. I needed a job where I could be available whenever Quon needed me. I turned to exotic dancing.

Five nights a week, I packed my workbag, carted my children to childcare, and went into the building with the neon lights. I sold my pride for dollar bills; my dignity for ten dollar lap dances; my soul for a chance to pay rent in the VIP lounge. No one should feel like they have to do the things that I've done to take care of their family. As mothers, we do what we have to do to survive… And survive, we did.

They took Quon out of the classes for the mentally retarded and mainstreamed him. He sat in regular classes with his non-disabled peers for most of the day. He had special group classes where he worked on things like reading comprehension and math. The Education Board thought that including kids with special needs, or inclusion, was a better way of educating them. I found that Quon couldn't keep up with the rest of the students. He had a difficult time staying focused and understanding the long lectures during the school day. When it was time to do homework, he couldn't reproduce the work that was demonstrated earlier. I sent back his work with my notes scribbled on the top of the sheet stating: "unable to complete on his own."

Quon made A's and B's in his classes. I scheduled meetings with his educators because I was not sure what his grades were based on. He clearly did not understand the assignments and didn't turn in homework. What exactly was going on in his class? They invited me to sit in his classroom and observe. I noticed Quon staring out the windows, playing with pencils, and not participating in classroom discussions. I tried not to cry as he sat there staring into space.

Soon after that, I withdrew him from school and decided to homeschool him. I knew I could do a better job than those "speaking at him" daily. It was a beautiful time of bonding. I created teachable moment every chance I could. Walking around the lake was physical education and biology. Trips to the store were handling money and socialization. Preparing meals included lessons on math and daily living. This may not have been a formal education but we were winning at life.

The next year the school contacted me. They revamped their special education department and invited me to observe their new classes. Students were paired with aids who had specialized training on the child's needs. I noticed individual accommodations with reading comprehension. Breaks, timeouts, and awards were allowed. I would like to think I had something to do with the changes but it wasn't confirmed. I was satisfied so I allowed him to return to public education.

Parents of children with special needs are fighters. We fight with society to end things like the "r" word and commenting on outbursts and behaviors when we are in public. We fight with family members who don't understand that traditional ways of parenting won't work on our child. We fight with the school systems for the same rights as the non-disabled students. There were days when we were exhausted from fighting and we just needed someone we could "tag in" to fight for us. That person for me was my son's fifth grade teacher.

Ms. Armstrong was and still is one of the greatest advocates for children with special needs that I know. Her classroom was a place of refuge where students were treated with respect and dignity. She took her students on trips, celebrated their victories, and invited their families to holiday lunches. Most of those expenses were paid out of her own salary. She was always available to answer questions about the classes, the future, or if you simply needed a shoulder to cry on. I never wanted Quon to leave her classroom. I didn't know what I would do without her wisdom and understanding. I solved that problem by making her my best friend.

One of the biggest challenges I faced when Quon entered high school was his path to graduation and what that would mean for his future. We had several different options: (1) The standard diploma for student with the required number of credits, GPA, and passing all standardized testing; (2) Certificate of Achievement given to students who perform to the best of their ability but didn't meet the standard requirements for the standard diploma; (3) Occupational diploma for students enrolled in the vocational program. I met with all the members of his educational team. We discussed our goals for his future, his current competency levels such as reading comprehension, math, and reasoning and options for placement. I wanted him to have his independence, to take care of himself, and became gainfully employed in case I wasn't able to be around to look after him. I didn't want that responsibility for his little sister. We decided to focus on daily living skills and vocational training for the remainder of his schooling. He was enrolled at the career center the following year. Despite not officially graduating with his class because of his extended educational plan, he was allowed to participate in the ceremonies and walked with his class.

Quon looked handsome in his cap and gown and tears streamed down my cheeks when they announced his name. I know I screamed louder than any other parent in the packed arena. A moment of sadness cast a shadow on the celebration when I looked at the two empty seats beside me. My parents didn't attend his graduation. We had an argument over his graduation party and they decided to stay home. I was hurt but found peace because Quon didn't know that they opted to miss on this glorious event.

After the ceremony, Quon began vocational training.

I saw Quon flourish. He improved on the skills he had like counting money, cleaning, and cooking and worked on some things that needed improvement like communication and self-advocacy. He ran the school snack shop and worked independently at Safeway Foods grocery store and Marriott Hotel. When Quon came home from school he told me about his day. I loved watching the excitement on his face as he recalled each event.

In the middle of his final year of schooling I received a job offer in a neighboring state. This was an opportunity to better provide for my family. I accepted and commuted four hours there and back. I used that time to speak to his new school system about Quon's needs to ensure they would be able to accommodate him before we relocated. I inquired about transportation, vocational training, and transitional service post high school. They assured me that there wouldn't be any issues with transferring his Individual Educational Plan to our new County. None of that was true. I immediately regretted the decision to relocate. They refused to provide transportation because he was close enough to the school to walk. They didn't take into account that he wanders, doesn't ask for help when needed, or was unable to avoid unsafe situations. I mentally pulled on my boxing gloves and began to fight the school system.

I received an email from the school principal informing me that Quon was no longer entitled to special education services in the entire state. They cited a state code that reserved the right to deny enrollment to any student after the age of 21. I was devastated. They knew Quon's age when I began the relocation process. I just accepted a brand new job and I couldn't leave him alone for 8-10 hours a day. I called every agency asking for assistance. No one could help us. I had no choice but to quit my job and go back on public assistance. I broke. The weight of my life snapped my spirit. I cried for hours. I cried over every job loss due to inefficient available care and absences from doctor and therapy appointments. I cried for the two marriages that ended from the overwhelming stress that comes with having a special needs child. I cried because Quon deserved better than this.

Quon is now 25 years old and is still on the waiting list for services. In the state of Maryland where we live there are over 10,000 individuals with intellectual and developmental disabilities waiting for services such as community services, day services, skilled nursing services, and integrated living services. I am currently developing a website to assist families in finding alternative ways to receive the services they need. I hope that no family who fought their way through the school system will have to wait while their family member sits in front of the TV while their skill are lost.

There are times as a parent when you realize that your job is not to be the parent you always imagined you'd be, the parent you always wished you had. Your job is to be the parent your child needs, given the particulars of his or her own life and nature.

–Ayelet Waldman

I wish I had a nickel for every time someone asks me, "How do you do it?" It's not a choice to me. It's my duty as the parent of a child who has special needs. I'm a warrior for my son from the time I wake up to the time I fall asleep but even warriors lose battles and fall short.

Quon hasn't changed since school. He's 25 and waiting on services like the other thousands of adults waiting on services. However, I'm not waiting on services. I'm creating opportunities for him and others like him.

These are some of the lessons I've learned and work on daily to keep me motivated on this journey. It's my hope that my experiences will assist you with your journey.

1. Allow yourself to go through the grieving process and know that there will be days when you wish things could be different. I still cry and Quon is an adult.

2. You don't have to know everything about your child's disability and you don't have to try everything that's out there. I tried it all and became overwhelmed. Find a trusted source and try a few things. You may find the best therapy is love and acceptance.

3. Trust your instincts and realize that experts don't always know best. I'm relieved that I didn't listen to my first pediatrician and institutionalize Quon. I would have missed the opportunity to assist him in growing into the happy, sufficient adult he is today.

4. Find a support system. You can't always count on your family or spouse to understand your feelings. I have a group of mothers that I can call at any time for any reason even if it's just to have a glass of wine for an "adult time out."

5. Celebrate your children. They are more than their disability. Take them out. Cheer for them. Be silly. It's good for them and for you.

6. Never stop fighting for your child. They deserve to be treated fairly by the world.

BE BOLD, BE RESILIENT, BE GREAT...BE YOU!

BY FELICIA R. SHAKESPEARE

"I've learned that people will forget what you said, people will forget what you did, but people will never forget how you made them feel."

–Maya Angelou

As a young girl growing up in the city of Chicago I knew that I would go to college. I did not know how I would get there, but I just knew I would. There was no blueprint or framework to glean from. See, no one in my family had done this before, at least no one that I had immediate access to. I would be the first and only in my immediate family to make this happen. Some would describe this as *knowing in your knower*, your very inner being. To go from *nothing to something* on any level can rank right up there as a miracle in my mind. It seems as if my entire life's story has, in its totality, added up to be a conglomerate of many miracles. I've always succeeded in all my accomplishments, against all odds. Most things have not come easy.

When looking back, I entered college not having a complete grasp or handle on my major; I just knew I was going. One inkling of a sign in the beginning was that I did feel an interest to teach, but I wasn't completely sold on it. By then I'd gained professional working experiences that greatly peaked my interest. In particular, those in a business environment.

Growing up, I was very fortunate to have a great relationship with both my mother and father. My parents early on stressed the importance of education to my brothers and me. We didn't have many possessions growing up and although socioeconomically considered the working class, by all accounts the bond that we shared as a family unit money could never buy. We had each other and there is no purchase price that can be placed on that. We lived life; how? Together.

Looking back now I feel we were rich in so many other ways. My parents were very traditional in the way that they raised their children. They would not allow society to replace what only they could impart to us. You talking about making lemonade out of lemons; we were well maintained as a family. My parents literally made sure that we ate our meals together purposefully and consistently just in our day-to-day lives, we did everything together. We were certainly inseparable. The situation wasn't perfect. I realize now how all of those life experiences shared, both good and bad, created an indelible imprint on who I was becoming as an adult. We had a roof over our head and food in our bellies. I don't care if it was just beans and cornbread.

I clearly remember our tiny one bedroom apartment on the west side of the city. Mom and Dad converted the living room into their bedroom. I don't know exactly why, but they were so nice and willing to give my oldest brother and me the bedroom. When my baby brother was born, I had to move over. We lived in that apartment from the time I was an infant until I entered the second grade. My parents provided structure. We were in bed super early because a good night's sleep was a must with school the next day in the Shakespeare household. We played hard together, too.

There were countless times we would be running through the apartment—the men versus the ladies—in a tag style game known as "it." We went to the park, museums, and beaches all the time. Why? They were all free. The two things in our home that I clearly remember were non-negotiables for my brothers and I was respecting God and respecting adults as if they were God. My parents grew up highly regarding education and the value of the teacher's voice. Because there was no silver spoon, my siblings and I attended the public neighborhood school system.

My parents did an excellent job managing their family but they could not shelter my brothers and me from the harsh cruelties of life.

By the time I was in the third grade I was bullied so much so, that my father had to take off work and come to the school to deal with the matter. There was a girl who insisted on trying to physically fight me almost every day. I was not that kid, but I was taught self-defense. I remember years later running into an old male classmate from that same elementary school and after some reminiscing, he told me how many of the kids hated me because I had a mother and a father at home. Learning this just blew me away. Not liked because I had two parents that cared about me? That made no sense to me, but I did have to process the thought because it was their truth and looking back at the various situations I had endured the pieces to the puzzle began to come together. Hearing this, even as an adult, made me a little sad.

When the bullying was happening then, I did not realize how much it was affecting me internally and shaping how I saw myself. I had to learn years later that the state of mind of those individuals had little to do with me. There was not one thing that I could have done differently, other than not be born.

Unfortunately, sometimes people want to make us feel like we should not have certain things if they don't have it. Sometimes people would want to make you feel like you should have never been born. Because I hadn't matured enough to recognize my own value, I started to think that something was wrong with me. This took a toll on my self-esteem. I felt like something was wrong and those feelings started piling on from a tender age through my young adult years. I did not call it jealousy then, because I did not process jealousy as wanting what another has that you don't. See that's the mature, adult definition. I dealt with the "why don't they like me?" or "what did I do wrong?" perspective.

I started to internalize a negative image of myself all because of what others thought of me. You cannot let the poor opinions of others be the basis of how you see yourself. Creating these negative images of myself absolutely did not make for the right ingredients for a growing girl or a budding young woman. But when you are the first-born and only girl, some things you learn to suppress and just go on. That was my personality.

This caused feelings of rejection, which affected my self-esteem so deeply that I would experience bouts of depression as a child. My heart ached. I fought through it to survive. Thankfully the core people in my life loved me and helped me move forward. Also, the basis of my faith allowed me to get through it.

My parents, as wonderful as they were, let me know well in advance that there were no funds to pay for my college education. They made it clear if I wanted to go to college, I would have to make my own way. During my senior year of high school, I applied for a position with a local bank as a teller and I got it. This was my first real exposure to working in a corporate environment and it made me feel excited and proud. I was now able to glean skills that I may not have been afforded otherwise (there comes a great responsibility with handling people's money) and I started saving funds in order to pay my tuition. Once I graduated from high school, I knew that I wanted to be an education major. My love of learning started at a very early age. I would actually teach my stuffed animals until my first brother's arrival, and then he became my first live pupil.

I chose to take classes at a local junior college by day and working in the evening. I was able to pay for my first two years of college as a working/commuter student. Because I was still living with my parents at that time, I was able to apply a substantial amount of the money towards the payment of my courses. I started to feel that career wise I could go far within the banking industry. I was so intrigued with the banking business that I didn't go into the education profession right away. My boss was very encouraging and my performance reviews were great. I found my niche and climbing the corporate ladder appealed to me. I enjoyed working for such an awesome company. Their approach to employees was sensitive and caring and what intrigued me most about banking was the organization of the particular bank where I worked. I was like a sponge soaking up everything I could about the banking world in order to become promotable. My company offered to pay for business classes. So this really put me at a crossroad of needing to declare my major. I was torn between sticking with education or going further into business. What should I do?

I felt at the time that teaching was a traditional enough profession that would always be there. And I felt the biggest barrier of me becoming an education major would be going through the student-teaching process. I could not fathom how I would be able to take off a year from work since I was responsible for funding my own education. At the same time I really enjoyed this business stuff and I was doing well. I made the decision to complete my studies and declare my major as an undergraduate student with a focus on business administration. I had hopes to make a transition into my new and exciting career once I graduated from college. In my senior year, with only one more class to complete, I went to the college career center and located five jobs that caught my interest. The company that was number one on my list called me about one month later. I was ecstatic when I received that call on a Sunday afternoon via my old school answering machine.

Their office was located ten minutes from my home and they offered me the salary that I had hoped for. I knew based on the company's size, there should be ample opportunity for me to grow professionally. I was hired for the position even with one semester and one class to complete before graduation. That was unprecedented, because rarely does any company hire someone who has yet to complete their degree.

As fate would have it, not only did they hire me, they paid for my last class. In my seven years there, I was promoted four times.

What was unique is each position was created due to company growth. In other words, no one had done those jobs before.

Little did I know, many of my first encounters of the subtle woes of the corporate world and all attached to it were about to be unleashed upon me with a vengeance. The glass ceiling, overt acts of discrimination, and a sometimes hostile work environment, simply because I was "degreed" surfaced their ugly heads. I was denied job training in my new position although management had blatantly requested my colleague to train me. I remember her never getting around to train me on anything for days. There was always an excuse. Many times she would just ignore me and not even speak to me for hours at a time although we sat in the same work area.

These experiences became another brutal awakening that life can be full of surprises, no matter the position you're viewing it from. There were unsolicited assaults on my character and my dignity, but I was a fighter. See, at that juncture, most individuals were standardly being hired to work for the company on a temporary basis from a contracted agency, with the potential to become permanent. There were no guarantees, but the chances to be hired were high.

When it was learned by some in my department that I had not come in the door as a temporary employee but permanent, the venom started to flow. Instantly it became a hostile work environment that I would have to endure for the next few years.

In complete confidence a few years later, I was informed by my co-worker who happened to also be a manager and friend in the company that I, along with one other female employee were being grossly underpaid compared to our peers based on a salary analysis. This information had been shared in a regional manager's meeting. When she heard I was one of the individuals who's name surfaced on the report, she felt compelled to let me know what was happening so that I wouldn't remain in the dark. Both myself and the other individual were discreetly placed on a work promotion plan not many days after I learned of this information. My direct manager never told me the nature of what had really happened behind closed doors. She simply lead me to believe that it was my time to soar elsewhere, and she encouraged me to seek new opportunities elsewhere with her full support as there were no immediate openings where I was. Even though my manager and I had become quite close – almost like a sister, she never came clean about the details even after I located a new position and I never voiced any knowledge of the situation. I just moved on. This required an upward shift in position.

So the search was on, I received an offer that took away my breath. It was where I wanted to go. The struggle I thought was ending, but not so. The gritty pieces of what I had to endure as an African American woman continued to surface. Words cannot convey the deep isolation and sadness that accompanied my journey. It's like being out in a huge ocean trying to find your way, when you're young and don't understand the dynamics of where to go, and how to navigate. I felt like I needed something I didn't have. I had to be resilient if I was to rise and keep my head above the water.

At the end of the day the major struggle was over, but in it all, I questioned whether this was something I wanted to continue to do. I had to be willing to step back, take a reality check, and see things for what they really were and to be a risk taker knowing it all may change.

There was one major problem though. Every year I was on edge, wondering if I would make the cut, and every year I knew layoffs were coming. A review of the budget changes in the ranks became unnerving too often leaving you wondering whether or not you would be able to keep your job. I didn't initiate change. I didn't plan for it, and I didn't want change, but I came to a point in my career where change found me due to the downsizing and surpluses that took place.

After being there seven years, almost to the day, it happened. A change had come.

I had a conversation with my mother one night and told her that I felt I would not be with this company much longer. She encouraged me to "ride it out" but literally the next day after speaking to her, I received a phone call from my manager stating that the department in which I worked was being downsized and my position would be eliminated. I'd at first sought out job leads within other divisions of the same company. After seemingly little to no success over a period of time, I decided it was time for me to go. I'd felt something was about to happen, but I did not know it would happen to the degree it did. It became an involuntary separation for me because every door I had tried to go through was not opening for me at this organization. I had to step back and do some praying. "Now what am I supposed to be doing next?" was my question to God. I had to listen and really hear for the right voice to speak.

I believe God will use anyone or anything to speak to you, and I had to be open to hearing Him through His vessels. My father, in the midst of all this, reminded me: "Felicia, didn't you really want to teach at first?" He was referring to when I was entering college. Teaching was my first love. Then he suggested that it might be a good time for me to reconsider teaching as a potential career move. It hadn't even registered as a thought before that moment, but I didn't just hear him, I heard him—I really heard him.

So, I started going in the direction to pursue teaching, Once I did, everything came together. Literally everything! I researched which tests to take and sought out a master's program. I then sought out a local university that was five minutes from my home that had not resonated with me originally. It was no struggle getting accepted there as my undergraduate degree had met all the necessary requirements for me to get in. I decided then in my heart and mind that no matter how long it took, working any job, I was determined to do whatever was necessary to go into the field of education. I had a made up mind.

After being officially accepted to the master's teaching program,' within two days of my college orientation, I received a voicemail from my advisor that a program would be announced on campus that weekend and she felt like I was a good candidate for it. We eventually stopped playing phone tag and she in turn provided all of the details for that upcoming information session. On the day of the presentation as I sat there listening, I started thinking to myself, *I've done all of the things that they are requiring in order to enter the program. I've taken the tests and I've been accepted to the college.* I mentioned this to one of the persons I thought was just helping out that day who ended up being the Assistant Superintendent of Schools for one of the program school partners. When I explained that I had done most of the things already, he asked me to come with him. He moved me to the front of the line, from forty something to like number six. Preparation had met opportunity.

You must be ready. I was interviewed on the spot, along with thousands who were also applying. After some weeks had passed, I learned that I was chosen as one of the 22 candidates selected. The program ended up having 12 of those 22 individuals who actually met all the requirements. I referred to us as the 12 disciples.

This accelerated program would allow me to finish my degree in half the time. I was elated to learn this. That was in February 2003, the month I had lost my Godfather to cancer, so this news indeed came at the right time to lift my spirits. I could move forward by focusing on something new as I healed from this loss. But the greatest hurdle was to come.

As I moved forward, completing one course at a time, the following February 2004, my world was turned upside down again. I abruptly and tragically lost my father. I was literally half way through my program, teaching as an intern when the school office sent someone to cover my classroom so that I could take a call from my family in the main office. My heart sank as I learned my father was being rushed to the hospital. My youngest brother who had called me at the school with the news reassured me that everything was okay and to just meet the family at the hospital. He really didn't have any idea that the worse had already happened. The ambulance had went on to the hospital with my father, but my family were behind at the house being questioned by the officers who had arrived on the scene with the ambulance. This was a very small town. The hospital was in the next town over, just minutes from my school, so I literally beat the ambulance's arrival.

But after waiting and waiting, I headed around the corner to question the nurses at the emergency room station and insisted on knowing my father's status and whereabouts. See it should not have taken this long for his arrival to the emergency room knowing the distance between the hospital and my parent's home, based on the time I had received the call. The somber looks immediately took over their faces when I gave his name. Something in me right then knew. They asked if I could wait on the doctor who would come and speak with me.

So I went back to the waiting area. Moments later a doctor and nurse began walking towards me. Here I am alone at the hospital and the next words were, "I'm so sorry to tell you..." My heart felt as if it were literally being ripped out of my body in that moment. A deep cry came from the bottom of my soul as I was given the news. Inconsolably I wailed right then and there and fell in the nurse's arms. I was at a deep loss.

I was immediately catapulted into indescribable pain, coming face to face with grief. After barely pulling myself together, I called to tell my mom, but she already knew. She and my brother would eventually arrive to the hospital. After speaking to her, I started calling everyone else I thought needed to know right then. My older brother and wife who were still en route. I called my pastor and my school program director as I was scheduled to be in class that evening. I was in total shock and pandemonium. A portion of my heart was gone. I will never forget that my program director, after learning my family had not yet arrived, made her way to the hospital just so I would not be alone. She sat with me until my family arrived. I will never forget what she did for me that day. My daddy was gone. The one who'd even encouraged me to enter teaching. I was a daddy's girl. My entire family would be changed forever beginning that day.

Dad had been all of our support system, especially for Mom, his wife of thirty years. In one moment everything changed. I not only had to continue on to finish my degree, I had to pick up the pieces quickly. One was passing the teaching certification test within a week of the funeral services in order to receive my licensure. That was no small feat. I literally thought I had nothing left in me on the day of the test. My mind was fogged with the loss I was experiencing, but I dug deep and after saying my prayer, somehow I passed. My inner self (both my resilience and my faith) took over.

In the coming months I would assist my mother with all pending legal affairs while I coped to bring some normalcy back to my day to day living. It was a treacherous time to say the least. But somehow I found the inner will and strength to plow on through such a difficult time in my life. I did complete my degree program in June that same year with all A's and one B. What propelled me forward the most during this time was not only my faith, but somehow I felt I was keeping a promise to my dad. I knew that he would have wanted me to move forward and finish. His investment of encouragement and guidance would yield the intended results of me going on to fulfill my dream and my purpose to teach at many levels. It was finally finished!

I'd since gone on to do some amazing things in the field of education. I was selected for the *Shining Example* teaching award less than two years of completing that degree. It was not long after I was afforded opportunities to appear on major television news networks and print publications to tell my story of becoming a career changer. This one move or shift afforded me countless opportunities that had I not made it would have not otherwise been possible. I've truly been blessed!

I was born to write and teach. My ultimate goal as an author and teacher is to provide the expertise that I have attained in the areas of coaching and training though my company, Integrity International.

Change is imminent and inevitable, whether you welcome it or not. I choose and welcome change that is necessary to allow me to further grow and develop in the gifts and purposes for which I've been created. As I prepare myself for many more transitions, I've learned through my experiences that there are certain non-negotiables that must exist in your life in order to receive the results you want. Those non-negotiables are hope, faith, love, dedication, and most of all an inexplicable resilience. You must never, ever give up.

I guarantee that sometimes, right when we are nearing some of the greatest breakthroughs in our lives, something will seemingly go haywire. This is not the time to quit! There is never a time to quit! You must also be willing to change your perspective about how *you* are seeing the activities in your life.

So I challenge you to take a much closer look at your life and all of the compartments it's made of and do a real honest inventory of yourself. How are you really seeing the different parts of you? If you're being negative, change your words and thoughts. Fill your mind and thoughts with the positive. If you're being wasteful, change your habits. Don't waste your time, your energy, or your money on things that are not a part of your purpose or that just don't matter. You have to see your life like it needs to be seen.

First you must change your outlook or perspective in order to have the life that you want. The way you think affects everything. It's not what you see, but it's how you see what you see. So as you begin to see yourself as an overcomer, you will become one. This becomes true perspective. You must also begin to envision yourself living the life that you desire. There is a quote that eludes to the fact that if you continue the same actions, but expect different results, that is truly considered insanity. Getting the results you desire does not only require you to assess your own actions in order to make the necessary changes. This thinking also begins the process to help you move forward. You must however commit to the process. Another critical component is that you must have faith. Faith is not seeing the tangible, but faith expects what may seem impossible. How many stories have you heard of someone beating the odds? Whether it's cancer, a debt, a career move, we must take steps to believe. You must learn to walk by faith and not by sight! What you're "seeing" can change at any moment. Life is very unpredictable, so why not believe for the best? Finally, in order to move forward you must be willing to let go of the past. Letting go of the past is a bold step to becoming who you were meant to be. You must be open to new possibilities, and looking back at past circumstances will keep you from doing that. Looking back can be a distraction. When you become bold enough in the process of letting go and start to move forward, you begin releasing those residues of pain of the past hurts in your life. When these actions are taken, then and only then will you position yourself for greatness. So I say to you: be bold, be resilient, be great…but most of all become the "you" that you were intended to become. Shift.

HAPPILY EVER AFTER

BY CHRISTINE NORMAN

"And we know that in all things God works for the good of those who love him, who have been called according to his purpose."

–Romans 8:28

I have always loved happy endings—in the movies and real life. And not just the regular run of the mill boy meets girl happy endings, but the extraordinary, "boy meets girl, girl moves away, boy searches the universe going through unimaginable means to find the girl" happy endings. The kind where the boy changes his whole life, swims across oceans, and even fights the lions, tigers, and bears (oh my) all for the girl. Not only that, but I love watching others win. If ever allowed to assign consolation prizes, the contestants would wonder if there were two winners and no real loser. I had a limited view of losses and had not come to know that sometimes you have to truly lose in order to win.

I now realize that my primary coping mechanism in life was trying to give to others what I so desperately longed for inside. I heard it said that we hear and see through our deepest need. Having sustained some knocks in life, I wanted happiness for others so badly because I feared that I could never have it for myself. God would have to teach me that I had to redefine happiness before I could ever have it.

Though my life had many of the "normal" components, so much of it felt empty. From the outside looking in, my family looked just like everyone elses. Some might have thought that it was even better than okay since I had my mother and my father. My physical needs were met, and I had more than a few of my wants. Still there were many scars and open wounds as a result of growing up in an emotionally unstable environment. My mother suffered from depression and anger for her entire life, and as a child I either interpreted it as my fault or tried to fix it by making her happy—a pattern that I would carry into my adult life and into other relationships. Her harsh demeanor started the inner dialogue that would plague my self-worth for many years to come. Though I had a loving and supportive father, I still wanted the love I could not get from my mom. I could never figure out if her criticism, nonchalance, and lack of effort concerning my feelings were covering her true feelings, or if she truly did not care; but either way, it contributed to the emotional trauma that I continually seek healing for today.

Though my mom was a teen mom, I never thought about the role her age played in many of the challenges that I faced with her while growing up. I now wonder if perhaps there were things she just didn't know how to handle because of her age. My mother had three girls by three different fathers, starting when she was 15 until she had me at 19. No doubt we were born out of her attempts to cope with the abuse and loss she faced growing up—abuse and loss she has never healed from. Her mother was verbally and physically abusive to her, so I guess she never learned to be nurturing. One of my sisters lived with her father and his mother. I wanted to be closer to my sisters but the way we were raised and the issues that we all face became bigger than sisterhood.

My extended family was just as complicated. I was too dark to gain the love or attention of my maternal grandmother. And since my father was much older than my mother, all but a few of his family members were dead long before I was born. So there were no real family bonds on either side. With no relationship with God and a growing self-esteem issue that I didn't know I had, I made a lot of poor choices. Again, I found myself with a life that looked like everyone else's outwardly, but I felt the effects of those choices inwardly and I carried a lot of guilt and shame. My relationship with my mom was not such that I could go to her with my life issues. I didn't have strong mentors in my life, and like so many young people, I thought I knew everything, so I didn't seek any out. I wish that I had known then how to reach out to those around me. There were people in my path and my family that I wish could have been closer. I wish that I had the courage or mindset to ask for guidance.

Though I was smart and accomplished in school, I went off to college not really knowing what to do. I did well and had fun, but I couldn't see where I was headed, and I didn't know how to communicate my fears to anyone. Not only had I never attended a college graduation at the time I was entering, I did not know a graduate up close and personal. I can now think back to three cousins that graduated from college, but I had no real relationship with them. I felt so insecure and inadequate.

I eventually met Leon, my daughter's father, while at Georgia State University. He was a campus police officer while I was a student. Even though my morals were relaxed, I vowed that I would never live with a man. Not getting the whole cow for free just made sense to me. However, I was living at home and going to school, but my home life was falling apart, and I was struggling to figure out what to do with my life. I moved in with Leon at 19. Shortly, thereafter I put school on hold. Not long after that, I was pregnant with Amber.

When Amber was almost a year old, I knew that I had to do more with my life. I was blessed to find good jobs, but I knew I needed more—the longing was still there. I married Leon thinking that would make us a family and save the relationship, but the marriage was over before it started. I knew that I deserved better, but since I was out on my own, I tried to make it work. This was my first adult relationship, so I had nothing to measure it against. We always had a good time, he just could not stay out of the streets.

Having Amber changed everything. I probably would have put up with his cheating ways as I always had, but I wanted more for her. Shortly after separating, a co-worker invited me to church and told me about needing a relationship with Jesus. One fall Sunday, I finally stopped making excuses and attended a gospel concert at her church. Not having spent a lot of time in church, I had no idea why the music moved me to tears. I didn't know how anything worked in the church, but I kept going and learning. One week before my twenty-fourth birthday, on December 18, 1994, I gave my life to Christ and things started looking up for me tremendously.

Eric had always been my friend. I met him when I was 20 years old, because we lived in the same apartment complex. Eric was funny, kind, and laid back and the nicest guy that I had ever met, with the warmest heart and smile. His smile still makes me melt and he is the calm to my storm. For years I tried fixing him up with many of my friends because he was such a great guy. Then one night, June 30, 1994 to be exact, he told me to come over because he had a friend for me to meet. He was that friend. We dated off and on from 1994 to 1999, but we always remained friends. We still describe ourselves as best friends today. Whether we did something, or nothing at all, our relationship has always been effortless. It was the kind of relationship where it didn't matter what we did, as long as we did it together. We had an undeniable chemistry and desire for one another. I always feared that if I did not end up with Eric, he would be the one love that would always have a place in my heart.

Through God's grace, Eric became my husband, and God changed Eric's life just as miraculously as He changed mine. God had used my failures, my poor choices, and all of the dysfunction that accompanied them to show me that His love and His blessings are not predicated on my goodness, but rather His goodness.

Though we got the family and marriage order a little mixed up (our son Christopher is in our wedding picture), we began building a solid life together. I returned to school and finished my bachelor's degree. I wanted my children to have their mother pave the way so that they would not face the same insecurities and uncertainties that I faced. My daughter heard the message loud and clear. Not only did she finish high school fourth in her class, but she also did two years of college in high school and got her Associates Degree one week before getting her High School diploma.

> *"Pain insists upon being attended to. God whispers to us in our pleasures, speaks in our consciences, but shouts in our pains. It is his megaphone to rouse a deaf world."*
>
> –C.S. Lewis

For most of my adult life until this time, I would not have complained significantly about anything. My new life in Christ had so blessed and changed my life that it far outweighed any difficulty.

Despite all that happened in the past and the regular challenges of life, my optimistic personality and my faith in God always caused me to see the glass as half full. Things were "almost" normal because it seemed that just when I decided to take my commitment to the Lord to a new level, many challenges came my way.

As I began the journey in seminary pursuing my Master's degree, our son broke his ankle then his kneecap. My husband fell off a ladder and had a minor fender bender. Then my daughter totaled her car, and her fiancé and high school sweetheart broke off their engagement. Nevertheless, I continued to persevere and press forward. I faced a few other ups and downs, got sick and had my five-month-old computer crash during the last week of classes right before the holidays in 2012, so needless to say I was desperately looking forward to a great new year.

Things had been going well in 2013, thankfully starting off uneventful, and I continued my studies again looking forward to my life gaining a sense of normalcy. But no sooner than I settled in, my son started having more challenges. I thought, *How much more, Lord?* Then on May 8, 2013, I glanced at my email during a break in a church service. There was an email from my daughter with the subject, "Please read before you go to church." I glanced over it as it was unusual to get such a long email from her, especially since she had just gotten home for summer break. I don't know if it was the topic or my heart's denial, but I could not understand what the email was saying. When I stepped into the hallway and read the email, I realized that my daughter was telling me that she had been raped.

My daughter had just suffered a heartbreaking broken engagement. She was a young lady who worked hard to lead others and be a light for Jesus on campus, and now this had happened to her. Hearing this after the fact, was the hardest part of this awful tragedy. Not only did I have to process what happened, I had to come to grips with the fact that I didn't get the chance to be there for her at that time. I didn't get to comfort her through the worst of it. I was not there when she was afraid. I could not reassure her of my love and of God's love despite this despicable horror.

I never asked God why He let this happen. I just believed that it had to be working for her good. I refused to believe anything else—I simply could not. I have heard others explain that in times like these they dug down deep inside themselves to find their strength. I give myself no credit. My heart and my head ached so badly that nothing was intelligible. All I could pray was, "God help me." All I could think was that this is working for our good. I know that God kept this belief in my heart to keep me from tormenting myself by asking why.

"How many things do we not walk away from because we see leaving as losing, so we would rather stay and die?"
                                        –T. D. Jakes

As the saying goes: when it rains it pours and my life felt like a level five hurricane. At the same time that I was trying to put things back together after this traumatic season for my daughter, the relationship with my mother was deteriorating, and I did not have the strength to deal with it. Just two months after I found out about Amber's rape, my mother would call me every few days about us moving together again. There were times when she called and I honestly had forgotten to think about it because I had so much going on. We had tried living together before unsuccessfully.

I have journal entries where I wrote out the pros and cons, trying to make a good decision.

I then let my mother move in with my family and me again, at a time when I was too vulnerable to make a rational decision. The differences in our demeanors were disrupting the peace I worked so hard to have in my home. I am the eternal optimist and always strive to have harmony at all costs. I was beginning to grow tired of the effort it took to coexist. When she didn't get her way she would literally throw tantrums and I would give in. Or she would find a way to manipulate me into doing something; much like she did to get me to allow her to move in with us the second time. I never had options with her and she often punished me with silence when I did not give her what she wanted—even as an adult. Since childhood, I had always been afraid for people to be angry with me or stop speaking to me, and for a long time this played a role in our dynamic.

Add to that, many of the people that I had been there for were no help to me, nor did they try to be. There were others who expected me to keep being there for them though it was all I could do to handle my own life. I so wanted someone who could be there for me for the long haul, but I feared that they would get tired of me crying. I wanted to let my heart break and have comforting arms around me until the pain was gone, but I could never let it all out because I didn't want to be a burden. I thank God that my husband was there, but he didn't always know how to help me and I didn't always know how to ask.

Everyone depended on me to be their sunshine, so I never wanted to be gloomy too long. My heart was breaking, but I was still trying to spread love and happiness, often from an empty place. Filling the cup of others when your own is empty is like trying to run a car without oil, a complete and utter breakdown is imminent. Though it would seem like that and what had already happened to my daughter was enough, my son was still hurting— nothing in life hurts like your children being in pain and you can do nothing to help them.

In the midst of everything else that was going on, God was showing me that it was time for me to leave the second church that I belonged to in life—and I was not ready. My refuge has always been the church. My surrogate family has always been the church. This church was where I learned of Christ and where I met the people who would show me a closer look at what I called true success. I looked at mothers and grandmothers that I admired, and I learned how to be the mother that I wanted to be. Church was the place where I made my character vision board. These people showed me how to be the things that I had never seen, and I did not want to leave again. I had served and ministered selflessly for years, but I needed someone to minister to me. I needed a soft place for all that I was going through. Not only that, but I also needed more hands on direction and development as I grew into new arenas that was not available at my church. I tried to explain what I needed but it wasn't well received. I was hurt and confused. I wanted to know how we could work things out but leadership was essentially saying if you are not happy here, perhaps you should find a place where you are happy. I felt I had no choice. Leaving is always more painful when your heart is bleeding, everything hurts more deeply. Holding on to something that has let go of you, hurts even deeper.

"Numbing the pain for a while will make it worse when you finally feel it."

–J.K. Rowling

Dr. Charles Whitfield says in "Healing Your Inner Child" that grieving one loss often forces you to grieve all ungrieved losses. Amber's rape blew the door open on all the pain that I had glossed over and pressed down. I found myself aching in places emotionally that I did not know I had. The problem with buried pain is that it always resurfaces. Buried pain, just like covered wounds, only festers. I prayed hard to handle it all. I asked God for more strength to deal with it all, all while my counselor reminded me weekly who I was ultimately responsible for and remind me that only I could remove myself from the cycle of dysfunction. I read the entire

"Boundaries" series by Dr. Henry Cloud and John Townsend. They also wrote, "Changes That Heal," "Necessary Endings," and "Never Go Back."

It took me reading all of those and so many more to realize that I absolutely do not have to stay in situations that do not work for me—ever! I matter, and I get to choose how I will live my life. I had begun to shut down emotionally, and it was a miracle that I did not lose my mind in the process. It took a while, but that truth set in. Despite what felt like bone-crushing and suffocating pressure, instead of breaking down, my true identity broke through. My soul blew a whistle and said enough was enough, and it did not matter who understood or agreed. The pain had awakened me from my slumber and I was not the same girl anymore. I proposed from that moment on to live differently.

Pain awakened me to everything that I was laying down and accepting and asking God to do for me. God is available to do all that we cannot, but He will not do what we can. I was asking him to send people out of my life when I had a mouth to tell them or legs to remove myself. I decided that I could no longer live my life for others or allow them to hold me captive in their drama. I broke away from everything that no longer served me. I decided to stop chasing people and begging them to love me, even if they were family. I know it sounds selfish, but there is a difference in being a help and a hindrance. Helping others should always make them more capable. If I give you just enough resources for you to get on your feet, then that was a help. However, if I give you so much that you never have to try to get on your feet, I become a hindrance.

I love being a generous and gracious hostess. A good hostess provides everything that her guests need and ensures that they are comfortable and have a great time. However, imagine hosting a party every night for a year. How long would that be fun? Funny when a parasite finds a place to live and breed, it too is called a host. I had become the source to others in so many ways, and it was now the time that I started to pour more energy into myself. While we do not keep score in relationships, there should be mutuality and reciprocity. Selflessness is one thing but we have to be really careful to notice when we are the only ones bringing anything to the table.

"…Weeping may endure for a night, but joy cometh in the morning."
                                                              –Psalm 30:5

The night is not always measured in hours, days, months, or even years. We also never know just how dark night can be. In those times, we comfort ourselves with the fact that morning is coming. I would never have asked God to usher any of this into my life, but I know I have been better after all that I have endured. Before my daughter's rape, I am sure that I might have carelessly thought that being stuck is a matter of "getting over it." I hate that phrase now. I now realize that getting over it is a process. Healing is not always a straight line—there are peaks and valleys in the process, but if you stick with it, develop practices that promote healing, and keep praying and believing, healing will come. I am learning to live courageously and intentionally because life is just too short for anything else. Out of the most tremendous chaos, amazing order and blessings can be birthed, and morning does come.

The Bible says that God gives beauty in the place of ashes in our lives. You don't get ashes unless something is destroyed by fire. The more fire, all the more beauty. Morning has come for my daughter as well. She graduated almost two years early with a Bachelors degree at the age of 20. She interned and trained at the top station in the nation, and is now a news reporter for the NBC affiliate in Augusta. She has moved forward, and I am learning to do the same. She says that I strengthen her, but she strengthens me in return.

"When you learn, teach. When you get, give."
                                                        –Maya Angelou

Through all of this, I have learned to investigate the pain in my life and I've learned what it has come to teach me. I have learned to release the fear, to begin hoping, trusting, and believing again, and to redefine my happily ever after. Walking in my truth daily is my happily ever after. Releasing the shame and guilt of my past and owning my experience for all that it taught me is happily ever after. Being brave enough to keep trying despite mistakes and setbacks, and loving despite utter heartbreak is happily ever after. Happily ever after is not some great achievement waiting to happen, but the small steps, tiny victories, and courageous changes that I am making along the way. Life is not being free of pain, but rather not forgetting the tremendous blessings that life holds despite the pain. I have also learned what to do with pain from the relationships that I lacked in my life. I can be to others what I desired for myself. Though we do not pray for pain, I pray that instead of fearing it, we courageously embrace the lessons that it can teach us and use it to serve and teach others.

THE OTHER SIDE OF FEAR

BY RYAN BLAIR-SMITH

"As we are liberated from our fear our presence automatically liberates others."

–Marianne Williamson

The day you find your happy place, is ultimately the day your life begins. Do you have a happy place that you just love to go to? You know, a place where you enter and immediately fall in love over and over again; a place that literally brings you peace every time you experience it. Well my happy place is nestled inside Barnes and Noble, where you will find me tucked away in the Starbucks area, sipping on a hot venti caramel macchiato and flipping through endless stacks of magazines and books—the Barista knows me by name. This place calms my soul, breathes life into me, and simply sets me free of worry. Through my experiences I've learned that we all need those moments of escape, moments where we can just be still and enjoy the beauty life has to offer. I must admit I haven't always been this centered, to be frank, I've struggled through some very ugly moments—moments of depression, thoughts of suicide, and fear of success—I'd much rather forget but these experiences have allowed me much growth and opportunity to bless the souls of others. I am fearfully and wonderfully made, I would tell myself when times got dark.

It was May 2003, my college graduation day, I stepped onto the big stage at Oklahoma State University and accepted my degree in International Business and Marketing. It was one of the most memorable days of my life. I remember like it was yesterday. There I was dressed to death, bold, beautiful, intelligent, and now armed with the credentials to prove it. College was the most eye-opening experience, full of adventure, ah-ha moments, life lessons, new relationships, and the best education ever. As I sat there on graduation day and reflected on my time in college, I couldn't help but to reflect on all the moments when I felt heartbroken in spite of my accomplishments.

I thought back to the day when the doctor said to a 10-year-old me, "Soooo Ryan, why do you eat so much?" That question would haunt me through my teen years, all the way through college, and led to a lot of self-doubt I would have about my capabilities. I think I experienced every emotion possible in college while trying to figure out what life would be like after. For the most part I was an upbeat, gentle, bubbly, and resourceful woman but that didn't mean I didn't get angry, disappointed, or fear the unknown. I often remained optimistic but some circumstances caused me to fear the other side especially when it came to the many roles I held while in college. I was heavily involved in numerous student organizations, sometimes to the point of overkill, and functioned as a resident assistant, otherwise known as a *dorm mom*. I must admit there were times I should have said no, but feared letting others down or becoming bored with myself. Even though I had a life-long struggle with my weight and sometimes used food to fill voids, I continued to push myself by entering pageant after pageant, even winning Miss Black OSU. Was I searching for acceptance from others? Did I need to hear from others that I was beautiful because I didn't really believe it myself? But when we take a step forward in faith, we open new doors. Winning Miss Black OSU gave me the opportunity to teach others and myself what real beauty is. Yet still I had doubts. And even though I kept up with my heavy class load in college, a bad break up with my high school sweetheart had me devastated for a while and I couldn't picture my future without him. But I survived our break up and as painful as it was, it taught me a lesson on perseverance and faith I might not have learned until much later in life.

Although a lot of people might not have known it, I was often paralyzed by fear. I was surrounded by it so much I gave it an identity and named her FEARlicia. She came with a hefty price tag, and boy have I been writing a fat check for more than 10 plus years. The relationship with FEARlicia was a debilitating one I often couldn't shake. She ruled every aspect of my life, from the doctors telling me I would never conceive and successfully carry a child—me accepting their *expert advice,* to the anxiety I felt when thinking about being successful. So I stayed stagnant; fear of leaving my hometown, the familiar, for an adventure of a lifetime to speak and travel the world.

I stayed home, *comfortable,* and among the familiar. Familiarity became a fear magnet and we were connected at the hip.

FEARlicia told me that I wouldn't amount to much and I believed her. After all I was a girl from a low-income, single parent home.

When she reminded me of my humble beginnings, I would often hear the whispers of my mother's voice telling me, "You are the poorest rich girl that I have ever known." That was her way of reminding me that my worth shouldn't be measured by the stuff I owned. My mother knew that wealth wasn't derived from financial gain only, but also by the matters of the heart. While we didn't have it all, we had each other and I was rich in that regard. My mother often asked me, "Do you believe what you tell other people? Do you believe for yourself, that you were designed for greatness, or are you just telling others that? I soon recognized that joy still exists and my heart's desires were within reach if I simply believed and did the work.

My home girl FEARlicia told me that as a mother and wife, I was selfish for desiring things outside of my family. There wasn't enough time to become great, I should've lived my dreams before getting married and having children, no one would listen to me, and I didn't have a calling on my life—I couldn't even encourage myself. Every single time I pursued my purpose, roadblocks appeared in the form of procrastination, self-doubt, worry, comparison traps, and worrying about the opinions of others.

My epiphany came when I sat down to talk to my five-year-old daughter—my first born—about living with purpose and dreams. I went into the conversation confident and ready to educate her on the joys of living on purpose and not just merely existing. But I quickly got a rude awakening. I started by asking, "Do you know what Mommy's purpose is? What is Mommy's dream?" She didn't truly have an opportunity to respond to any of my questions, as I let them roll off my tongue like a drill sergeant, expecting rapid-fire responses in return. I was too excited about my purpose and wanted so desperately for her to get it. She suddenly blurted out with excitement, "You're a cell-phone girl!" I thought to myself, *I'm a WHAT?* Trying not to show my distaste for her response, I immediately give her a blank stare with one eyebrow raised and used the sweetest docile tone, asking, "Cell-phone girl?"

She was naively referring to my job at a cell phone company but at this point, my entire demeanor changed and my confidence had run out of the room. I wanted to hide under a chair and burst into tears. She was just sitting there looking at me with the biggest snag-a-tooth grin, proud of her answer and chest puffed out as I sat in a daze, heartbroken and riddled with disappointment. The most important person in my life had absolutely no earthly idea who her mommy was—it was simply devastating to think about. In my simple mind, if I had died at that very moment my life would have been in vain. I believed I'd failed at being a mother. I was not the role model that I thought I was or desired to be. I wanted to be my daughter's example, not some perfect stranger on TV—but ME!

Operating in fear had kept me from living my purpose out loud and my daughter confirmed my fear paralysis. At that very moment, I knew something had to change. I am not called to be a cellphone girl, of that I was certain.

My child didn't realize just how much she blessed me on that day. What initially broke my heart, knowing I wasn't her hero and she didn't recognize an ounce of what I was purposed to do, became my greatest blessing in disguise. The innocence of my daughter gave me my greatest life epiphany. I was created to serve women— help them uncover their value, pursue their passion, and be the woman they were destined to be. When I finally decided to be transparent about my life and my struggles I felt so liberated that I had a desire to help other women do the same. So, I spearheaded my first Women's Conference, "There's MORE to YOU!" I set out to create a conference that attendees would realize there was more to them than the surface things that they were operating in. Life was more than just being someone's wife or girlfriend, working a 9 to 5, and being a mom. It was important that they dug deeper and really pursued their purpose and passions in the midst of fear and showing up for others. I firmly believed that we must show up for ourselves before we show up for others.

I often shared with women that winning Miss Black OSU was far more important than a tiara, roses, and a title but it was about the truth that conquering fear brings. I wanted to encompass the true essence of beauty, from inside out. Furthermore, it was about creating a legacy, and fostering a culture of women who believe in who they were created to be. As a mother, it was important that my daughters and generations to follow understand the magnitude of going after your dreams—afraid and all! There's no level of success where fear is eliminated and it's important to understand it would be there but it was up to us to determine what we did with that energy. Will you allow it to paralyze or fuel you? I was determined to allow it to fuel me, igniting a new normal in my life—knees knocking and all.

I researched avenues to become a full time speaker and do vision boards again. I looked up various events and workshops that would keep me focused on my goal and came across Jonathan Sprinkles' Presentation Power conference. I invested in myself and received coaching from Mr. Sprinkles. I had four eye-opening days that allowed me to believe in possibility again. I stepped outside of my normal, introverted self and volunteered to jump on stage and present my truth—my *why*. It took me a few tries to get it right because I stood in the way of my own breakthrough, as my old friend tried to creep her way back in, but this time I wasn't having it.

As the words began to flow from my heart, tears streamed down my face. I did it! I finally divided and conquered fear and the audience's standing ovation was confirmation that my truth was alive and well. I no longer felt the weight of FEARlicia's insecurities. I no longer would dim my light to make others feel comfortable. I could feel confidence and courage flow through my veins and faith stood beside me. With faith standing beside me, it was time to graduate from the school of fear but this time with a degree in Freedom and Purpose. Obtaining this degree had to be a little more special than the one I got from OSU because it reminded me of the quiet moments spent with God, the moments He confirmed His promises over my life, and the gift I was to others.

My determination allowed me to continue evolving and new doors opened. I was centered and at peace with my journey. I knew I had to be kind to the universe and not be selfish with my gifts so I created a workshop and program titled *Dream Print: Vision Board Party*. I often refer to it as partying with a purpose, going from FEAR to FLAIR, *Fearless Living and Attracting Intentional Results*. Dream Print allows me to show women how to gain much needed clarity, write their visions, dreams and goals, and envision who they are created to be. To further challenge myself, I accepted opportunities to host, present, and facilitate workshops for women. I was in full throttle and a woman on a mission.

It was important that I foster a culture of women on a mission, women who encourage one another to create their own dreaming life. I wanted to share my top *5 Dream Tips* and lessons with you that I've learned along the way to greatness. Go be great and dream on!

Dream Tip One: Find Your Purpose Power— Know Your 'Why'

The Lesson: Think about the things that bring you the most peace, something you'd do without being paid. This is not the time to operate in a mediocre state of mind—clamming up and usher in the excuses. This is your time to accept the invitation. If you are playing small with your purpose, allowing life to pass you by— opportunities to pass you by; I urge you to stop and embrace the opportunities that come your way. Marianne Williamson says it best in my favorite poem: *"Your playing small does not serve the world. There is nothing enlightened about shrinking so that other people won't feel insecure around you."* Our Deepest Fear by Marianne Williamson.

You don't have to have everything together but once you step into it there's a power that comes from it. All the opportunities you are passing up may not come back around. Those missed opportunities are called opportunity cost as my friend, coach Jonathan Sprinkles says. Instead of playing small, start living life with FLAIR. The word FLAIR equates to a powerful simple truth. Your fearless action propels you to unleashing the power in your purpose. That power will open doors that will blow your mind and change your life. It is time for you to know you have more than enough inside of you and the best thing is, the world is ready for it. The things, people, and places around you are ready to receive all the unbelievable gifts and talents you were born with. The world is ready to receive a mark on it because of you sharing your undeniable greatness!

Bonus: Don't Drown. Take off the excuse life jacket to keep from drowning. That is exactly what I was doing, drowning in my excuses and I don't want that for you. Let's swim.

Dream Tip Two: Self-Interrogation— Ask Yourself the Tough Questions

The Lesson: Grab your journal or a piece of paper to jot down your responses to the following: Have I tapped into what I have been called to do? Am I walking in my purpose? Is there really more to me? Have I given life my all? Am I passing up opportunities without truly thinking of the pros and cons of the decision? Will I have regrets?

Ponder on your responses creating three action steps along the way. Once you start operating in your purpose you will see the power of it and its effects on those around you.

Dream Tip Three: Overcome and Embrace the Roadblocks In Your Life.

The Lesson: We all experience roadblocks, times in life where there are hurdles that we must jump in order to get to the other side. To overcome the hurdles, we must first recognize that they exist. Take a moment to write down three hurdles you currently face in your life, next write down two ways you'll overcome each of them. Remember to have a backup plan to the back up.

Dream Tip Four: Matters of the Mind— Make a Mental Shift

The Lesson: God sent Moses to help lead the Israelites out of bondage in Egypt to the Promised Land, which was a promised inheritance from God, a land that overflowed with milk and honey and of course a place where they (the Israelites) would lack nothing. They were simply ordinary people headed to an extraordinary new land and new way of life. Imagine being enslaved for hundreds of years like the Israelites, generations and generations of your family being commanded how to eat, sleep, breathe, dream, and move. One day you are set free from all the misery. I do not know about you but I would have laced up my tennis shoes and commenced to sprinting as fast as I could to get to that Promised Land. Unfortunately, that was not the case for the Israelites once they were released. It literally took them 40 years to make the trip that should have only taken 11 days. Talk about blocking your blessings! They were in a mental war. Even though they were free, they were trapped mentally. They often contemplated reverting back to slave mentality. Some simply gave up and died in the process and never reached the land. Just because they were on a journey through the wilderness did not mean their mindset needed to be in a "wilderness" state. Instead of commanding their freedom and showing their gratitude in advance, they decided to harp on their present with negativity. The mind is a powerful tool that can either help you succeed or be your demise.

Bonus: Create an affirmation and repeat to yourself each morning for 30 days. Your mental freedom starts with you and your language.

Dream Tip Five: Surround Yourself With Brilliant Minds

The Lesson: Surrounding yourself with brilliant minds is a critical piece in your dream shift process. You are more prone to being successful in your shift once you rid yourself of naysayers. The weeding process looks different for everyone but is a necessary component in creating a circle of greatness. It also can be difficult to go through. Here's my recommendation: incorporate people who are striving for more, will hold you accountable (tough love), and are authentic encouragers. Find them, trust me, they are out there, and they need you, just like you need them. You simply do not have time for negative people, they are distractions taking up valuable space and time.

Following these dream tips and lessons will assist you in conquering fear—making bold, unapologetic moves. You'll soon find yourself embracing your passion, and living out loud. I celebrate you in advance.

JOURNEY TO FIND ME

BY MIASHA GILLIAM-EL

"Becoming aware of yourself and the impact you have on the world is not an easy task. It is not for the faint at heart or weak of mind."

—Iyanla Vanzant

Have you ever wondered why life has dealt you the hand it has? Have you ever thought to yourself, *Why me?* My journey up to this point has not been easy. I was not born with a "silver spoon" in my mouth or had the benefit of overflowing opportunities. Most of my childhood was spent growing up in the inner cities of Baltimore. At the age of five, I quickly understood that I was not one of the lucky few that would enjoy an easy life. I was born to a mother who came from an extremely rough background. She was from a very large family where she had seventeen brothers and sisters in total. My grandparents were not well educated, but they worked hard to provide for their children which was not always easy.

My mother married young—not for love but to escape poverty. At the age of twenty-five she got married, became pregnant with me, and was separated from her family and the only environment she knew. My father was a soldier in the Army and presented so much promise. My mother assumed he was established and she looked forward to a different and better life than the one she was accustomed to. She set off on her journey from Virginia to Maryland, not knowing what lie ahead of her. Little did she know my father would prove to be controlling and liked to step out on the marriage more often than not. Their marriage was not a healthy one and I remember constant arguing and physical aggression. There was virtually no communication between the two of them, outside of the arguments.

My mother had a history of alcoholism and when unhappiness in her marriage set in, she quickly returned to her old hobby of drinking. As my father continued to commit adultery, he distanced himself from the marriage. My mother started hanging in the streets and exhibited a lack in judgment due to her alcoholism. I was taken to places, saw things, and sat in environments a child should not be. My mother had jumped from one abusive relationship to another looking for love. I watched my mother endure domestic violence for years.

Looking back on my life at the age of five, I had angels encamped all around me. Two of which were my godmothers who I loved dearly, Cat and Mrs. Pearl. They played the roles of both protectors and teachers. These women made sure I had meals, baths, and the ability to function as a child when my mother was incapable due to her disease of alcoholism. I don't blame or fault my mother for how I was raised because she did the best she could with the knowledge she had. And although she was an alcoholic, my mother had a magnetic personality and was one of the most generous people I knew and she made sure her children came first.

Once my mother and father separated, she was introduced to an older gentleman, who I came to affectionately call Mack. I admired him and the many things he taught me when I first arrived at his house, like how to cook. He also introduced me to a variety of foods I had never been exposed to. I was finally able to see what I thought was a loving relationship and I was happy to see my mother smiling once again. I had seen her sad for so long. Mack had children who were almost the same age as she was which was challenging at first, but as time progressed everyone loved her.

This house represented a new beginning for me. It was like I was given a new outlook on life—a fresh start. After about a year of getting adjusted to my new environment, at the age of six, the unthinkable happened. Someone who was well acquainted with the family molested me. No one knew what was going on but me. This went on from age 6 to age 11. I never felt so powerless in my life and I did not understand what or why this was happening to me. I was pinned in a corner on several occasions and told that my mother would be harmed or we would be kicked out because my step-dad, Mack, would not believe me. I never told anyone but my mother because my offender was constantly threatening me. My mother did not believe me or did not want to believe me. She told me I should stop making things up. After I shared with her what was happening and she did not help me, I felt I had nowhere else to turn. After all, my mother was supposed to be my protector.

Was I a "bad little girl" who deserved this? When this kind of thing happens to a child, he or she learns to detach as a survival mechanism. I learned to take my mind to other places during the abuse and this was one of the things I believed helped me to keep my sanity. Another thing that kept me sane during this time was my best friend, Raymonda. Without her and her grandmother, Mrs. Lorraine's, love, I don't know what would have happened to me mentally. My best friend and I would play together for hours and we would model her mom's clothing while her grandmother cheered us on. I can remember playing in expensive Max Factor make-up and it not being an issue. We watched horror movies, tore up the kitchen cooking, and reading for hours from her massive library. Here is where I learned to utilize my imagination through reading. It became my means of escape and I learned so much from just engulfing myself in books.

My childhood was not all bad. I enjoyed spending time with all my friends and playing in the garages with Latonya and Keith, two other childhood friends. There was one other thing that made me happy and that was the announcement of my mother being pregnant. My sister, Tanika, was born when I was six and I can remember doing her hair, dressing her like she was my doll, and her going everywhere with me. We were like two peas in a pod. My sister was with me even when I did not want her to go. I can remember her crying to go outside with me. I tease her now and tell her she was just going to spy on me for my parents.

I was eleven when the molestation ended, and even years afterwards my self-esteem was tarnished and I did not trust anyone anymore. Even though the perpetrator ended up dying, which stopped the abuse, holding this secret inside continued to eat away at my self-esteem. I had to learn how to interact with others again and try to piece my life back together, without even understanding what had happened or why. My life felt like there was a disconnect. I had learned to protect my mind by what I call "throwing things in the furnace."

This was a practice where I envisioned myself taking unwanted feelings and emotions that were boxed up and toss them in the furnace of my mind. It helped me to cope with and alleviate a lot of negative emotions that I dealt with like hatred, unforgiveness, and anger. I started to analyze things and ask myself how would I live a normal life now when I was anything but normal.

My life seemed to spiral downward for a couple of years, as if I was sinking deeper and deeper into despair, until a friend came into my life and brought me hope. She not only encouraged me but she pointed me in the direction of Christ. I attended church with her and learned about the Lord, using what I was learning to mend my broken soul and spirit. Church was a place I never thought I would have ended up because my mother and father never introduced me. For some reason I knew about God and who He was, but I did not know what He had to do with me.

There was an awesome youth fellowship and the church Faith Tabernacle was united and cared about the young people. I spent so much time with the youth in church that they became like family.

While at church I fell in love with one of the young men in the youth fellowship. I felt safe enough to let my guard down. We were together almost every day until I left for Talladega College in

Alabama. I was accepted as a Pre-Med major and I was so excited for change. My mother was so proud of me. Everyone in the neighborhood knew the name of the college and where it was because my mother went all out for me. I had everything I needed and more.

When I arrived at school I was really nervous about the fact that I had no relatives in Alabama and that it was so far away from home. I had never experienced being this far away before and I had no option but to succeed. While I was away at college my boyfriend and I called each other often to keep in touch. This was a very happy time in my life; I was in love and doing well academically. I had also formulated a close circle of friends who I could trust. Who could ask for more?

Everything was so close to perfection that I felt it was too good to be true. It was not long before I received the news from home that my mother was sick due to the fact that she stopped drinking without any assistance from the doctors. She was one of the bravest people I knew. Once I came home I saw the severity of the situation. My mother had memory loss and could not really take care of herself anymore. I was home the majority of the day with her and it presented me with such agony to watch her wither away slowly but I endured and remained strong for her. My mother was a fighter, but I knew she was giving up when she looked at me and said, "You can't continue to do this," meaning take care of her. She had grown tired.

My boyfriend was still in my life at this time and we began a sexual relationship. After about four months of being home, he unexpectedly proposed to me. We were so happy for the first couple of months until I became pregnant. Things spiraled downhill from this point. The love of my life abandoned me. He expressed that he felt I had trapped him and I could not figure out why he thought I would do something like that after knowing me for five years. Did he really believe I was capable of this behavior? This hurt me to my core and I was furious at the same time. I started to find out things like he had another girlfriend living with him. I found out the girl was his girlfriend because she called me on the phone when I paged him. When I tried to go talk to him he would not open the door or answer my calls. Like a crazy person I still kept trying because I did not want to believe things were truly over. I did not want to be alone, especially with my mother being ill and with me being pregnant.

At this time my now ex-fiancé's mom was my only support system. When I was five months into my pregnancy, I was at my mother's funeral. She lost her battle and died from cirrhosis of the liver. She was a true warrior and survived two months under the care of Hospice nurses. I knew she was tired, but I did not think she would actually leave us and die. I never told my sister, Tanika, but she was the one who encouraged me to be strong when it was supposed to be the other way around. I felt like my life was over at this point and I experienced times where I felt as if I did not want to live. What would I do?

During these times I felt everyone was so disappointed in me. My family had such high hopes of me getting married and becoming a doctor. I was on the verge of being put out by my stepfather because we were constantly arguing about my situation and how I had messed up my life. My stepfather finally did put me out and I had nowhere to go, but a couple houses down to a neighbors house. The house was awful and she had a dog that constantly barked at me when he saw me, therefore I remained upstairs until the owner returned home. This means I had to keep food in the room in order to eat. The dog stayed locked up in the kitchen.

My mother was deceased at this point but my now ex-fiancé's mom jumped right in and taught me all I needed to know about being a mother. She was there for me through so many rough times with encouraging words. She let me know I could make it through this trial with my faith in God. She encouraged me to go back to school and took every opportunity to assist with my son in an effort to help me be successful. She was at my house almost every weekend washing his clothes, babysitting, and helping to provide for him in any way I needed. She became my backbone and helped me to stand with strength and courage through all the nasty looks and gossip that followed me. I was so grateful God had placed her in my life.

I was so lucky to have two strong women showing me the way. My biological mother was my angel. She made sure my life was on track. I did not know how I would have made it through my problems without having my mother there to console me. It tested my faith in God. But I soon realized that even though He was not with me physically, God was always guiding and directing my path.

I wanted to become a nurse after watching my mother's situation. I wanted to help others even though I could not help her. I enrolled at Baltimore City Community College in Maryland. I was about 25 years old and wanted to be a Psychiatric Nurse because I loved psychology. Even though I was trying to get myself together academically and career wise, my mind was still weak. I had lost who I was and I was use to changing to become what others wanted me to be. In losing myself I became involved in one terrible relationship after another looking for love and security. I spent so many years in mentally and physically abusive relationships because I could not define who I was. I wanted someone to rescue me.

I felt like giving up so many times, but something within me would not allow it. I remained a fighter. I went to school and held down two jobs in an effort to provide for my son, Ja'Corey. He was my inspiration and motivation to be successful.

Over the next couple of years I worked hard to reach my goal, but it was not easy. I met my now husband, Everett, at a gas station and my life changed. We were driving down the street and caught each other's eye. We decided to pull over to the gas station and talk. As he was talking to me that evening I felt butterflies, it was like I already knew I had found my soulmate. He was so different than the type of men I was use to dating. He was into reading, heritage, and culture. He loved poetry and would spend hours reading it to me. Unlike all the other men, he spoke about family and wanting to do something to help the community. I felt like he was a visionary and wanted to build on the principles that would create a strong family. He was not out to just sleep with me and he actually cared about my thoughts and feelings.

The friendship continued to flourish and I pushed for an actual relationship. He had been scarred in a previous relationship and wanted to make sure I was the one he wanted to be in a relationship with. I spent a couple of months assuring him that I really wanted him in my life. We spent a lot of time together and really got to know one another. Everett was also great with my son, Ja'Corey.

After about six months of just seeing each other as friends, a commitment was made to begin a relationship. I was ecstatic. I finally found someone who loved and understood me. We had our first son together in 2004. I knew at this point I wanted us to be a family. Of course as we proceeded through our relationship there were many obstacles from previous relationships and children, but we made it through. In 2005 (two children later and I was pregnant with our first daughter) we were married. My wedding day was one I will never forget. I could now see the life I envisioned.

Seven years later during my fifth and last pregnancy in 2012 I began to understand my purpose for being on this earth. I experienced issues with swelling and my blood pressure. I was diagnosed with Pregnancy Induced Cardiomyopathy. This is when your blood flow backs up into your lungs causing your lungs to fail. On my last appointment I was sent to the Labor and Delivery floor of the hospital to deliver my son. They were afraid I would have a stroke so they administered Magnesium to prevent it. I felt fine after my baby was born but when I was leaving to go home I noticed my blood pressure was still elevated.

After two days of being home with my baby, my husband had taken my other four children to the bus stop on the morning of February 27, 2012. When I attempted to get out of bed, I immediately fell to my knees. I was experiencing Pregnancy Induced Cardiomyopathy. In other words, my blood was not pumping correctly and was backing up into my lungs rendering me unable to breathe. I was rushed to the hospital by ambulance as my life flashed before my eyes. I quickly realized who was in control and it sure was not me.

At this point I let go and focused on the promises of God. While in the emergency room I stopped breathing and my heart stopped for approximately 16 minutes. I was placed on a ventilator. I remained on that ventilator for two full days and on the third day I woke up. Zech 8, which is my church family, came together during this time and prayed that God would spare my life and that's what He did. I am so proud to be a part of my church family—they exhibit true unconditional love. They took shifts to make sure that my husband and children were well taken care of.

Another angel that takes no credit is my friend from nursing school, Tracie, who kept my husband calm explaining all the procedures and the processes of things in the hospital. That in itself provided comfort to him. When I left the hospital my will to live and my desire to fulfill my purpose was stronger than ever.

As I sat in my living room, God blessed me with the idea for my business, Herbal Delitz Cupcakes. I started this business in 2012 with the vision of making cupcakes that are both healthy and delicious. I incorporated some of the well-known healing spices into the cupcakes such as lavender, and they were delicious. I started on this venture because as a Nurse I see so many patients, who are young people, suffering from high blood pressure and diabetes. I wanted them to be able to enjoy the desserts they love without jeopardizing their health. I knew this would be an adventure finding the right branding so I appealed to those who are striving to make small, but healthy changes in their life. As I began to market my customer base expanded. People really loved to eat the cupcakes and gave them for gifts. The idea was and continues to be well received.

My gift has given me the ability to affect many lives and meet many people from various walks of life. God was always positioning me to be a leader—I just had to accept it and surrender. I now use every opportunity to uplift and motivate others. I try to educate others including my children on the importance of community building. Looking back on all the tribulation I endured, I had to will myself to be successful spiritually, mentally, financially, and physically.

Today I wear many hats: I am a wife, a proud mother of nine children, an elder in my church, a registered nurse, and a business owner. I have three grandchildren and one niece whom I adore. I am a survivor of poverty, molestation, depression, domestic violence, and death. No matter what obstacles I faced I believed that I served a God that was greater. There have been many times when I wanted to give up, but there was an internal drive that kept me striving to reach my goals. The ability to draw from the faith within when you are going through trials and tribulations is essential. You must always put your best foot forward and fight for those dreams that you hold dear to your heart even when you are told they are unattainable.

I spent years surrounded by negativity. If I had a dollar for every person that belittled me and told me I would not be successful, I would be a millionaire. When you grow up in the impoverished inner city opportunity scarcely presents itself. Hope helped me to see past what my physical eyes saw. In 2007 I set out on a journey and in 2010 I graduated from college Cum Laude with an associates of science degree in nursing. I worked on a step down unit where I cared for patients preparing to go to heart surgery or were returning from heart surgery. I was one of ten students selected to participate in this nurse residency program in the state of Virginia. I quickly climbed the nursing ladder and after only two years I obtained a position as a Unit Manager on a 62-bed unit in a long-term care facility or what most people refer to as a nursing home. Out of the 62 residents, I was responsible for 18 skilled residents that were there for therapy only. Once they were able to complete care for themselves they could be discharged.

This was a different kind of responsibility and was very demanding. I received a $10 pay raise and I was able to enjoy the benefits of being a salaried employee. "…To whom much is given, much is required…" (Luke 12:48).

One of my biggest struggles to overcome was accepting who I am as a person and loving myself as the individual God made me to be. I had to learn I am uniquely and individually made for success. For many years I walked in the shadows of others including my family. It took time to realize that what I had to say was just as important as what anyone else had to share. God gave me a voice and I decided to walk out on faith and utilize all the gifts he has endowed me with. As I continue on this journey called life, I know the sky's the limit and as my elementary school principal use to quote William H. Johnsen saying, "If it is to be, it is up to me."

I challenge anyone who fears they cannot make it to put these steps in place towards success:

1. Have a vision. When you have a vision in mind, it pushes you to set goals in an effort to achieve that vision.

2. Surround yourself with successful people. Sometimes it helps to see what success looks like and realize it is within reach. Talk to and learn from successful people.

3. Expand your knowledge base.

4. Make yourself marketable.

5. Have the ability to dialogue with others in various arenas.

6. Don't be selfish with your blessings. Be willing to help others on your road to success.

7. Never give up. If you don't believe in yourself and your dream-no one else will.

Affirm this to yourself. Say it until you believe it and start to see a transformation in your life.

I will be who God says I am.

I will fulfill my purpose.

I will be a success.

I will uplift and edify others.

I will make a difference in this world.

I will not let anyone tear down my spirit.

I will not fall prey to low self-esteem or depression.

I will not doubt what I already know.

I will not give up.

I will not fail—failure is not an option!

If you are reading this, you know that nothing happens by coincidence. It's all a part of the plan for your life. Therefore, it's time for you to arise, position yourself, then take flight and walk in your purpose. Pull from your inner strength and press forward. "Trust God with your whole heart and lean not unto your own understanding, acknowledge him in all your ways he will direct your path." (Proverbs 3:5-6).

Remain faithful on your journey to reach your goals and don't let what you see happening around you become a distraction. Your dream and aspirations are within reach so remember who you are, step out on faith, and fulfill your destiny.

FAILURE ISN'T FATAL OR FINAL

BY PATRICIA JOHNSON-HARRIS

"I want to be a woman who overcame obstacles by tackling them in faith, instead of tiptoeing around them in fear."
                                                        –Renee Swope

Looking back I realize life's blows aren't reserved for adults. They have no respect for age or person. I had been a happy-go-lucky little girl enjoying ice cream at Coney Island when in 1975 life intruded and leukemia took my father, John Henry. I was eight and Ruby, my mother, was left to raise five children.

I am the youngest of seven and at the time of my father's death, two of my siblings were no longer in the household. My mother was a strong, caring, and loving woman who did the best she could to raise us with the little she had. Life was hard back then, even cruel at times. There was more month than money. Living on public assistance, my mother juggled as best she could, but at times having no food, we drank water just to fill our stomachs. Through it all my mother remained positive, at least that's my perception, because she always smiled, never raised her voice, and was there to give hugs and kisses when most needed. We didn't have much, but we had each other.

There were fun times. I remember going everywhere with my mother—I was her shadow. I guess being the baby had its advantages. I loved when it was just the two of us, whether it was going

239

to run a few errands, or going to church for Bible Study or choir rehearsal. It didn't matter. I just liked those special times we shared. I was happy but not so "go lucky."

Life intruded at eight and stole my "go lucky" when my dad died and at twelve my "happy" was taken away when my mother died. The last time I saw her was in the hospital. Having had a stroke she was trying, although not succeeding, to show me how to rock a baby in her arms as part of her physical therapy. My sister and I left the hospital, but by the time we arrived home and before we entered the house some of the neighborhood kids ran up to me saying—maybe asking, it's somewhat blurred—your mother is dead. Not believing or understanding because I had just seen her sitting up and talking, I went in the house only to be told again that she was gone. What now? What was I going to do? Where was I going to go? What would happen next?

After the funeral, the family stepped up to care for the five of us, but no one could take us all. I went to live with my oldest sister's family. It was difficult for me because I was not raised with my oldest sister and I didn't know her. I cried at night because even though we were related, I felt like a stranger. So two weeks later, I went to live with another sister. Her husband was an aggressive man and very strict. I wasn't used to living in a home where you had to ask for permission for almost anything. There was a lot of yelling as well and I was afraid to sleep. So, I didn't seem to fit in there either and went back to my oldest sister's family.

I'm not blaming anyone that I felt lost but it was a season of despair. I had shut down. Outwardly my appearance screamed, "I don't care." My grades plummeted. I was a mess. I wanted to run, but where to? I hadn't finished school and certainly couldn't support myself. I had been sheltered by my mother so the streets of New York terrified me. I had no desire to become bait to those who prey on runaways. Yet to remain in this state I would surely die.

Then one day a glimmer of hope looked back at me as I stared in the mirror. My homeroom teacher, Mrs. Hutchinson, told me that I was special and that my mother was watching over me and wanted me to be happy. She said that I was going to do great things in life, to keep doing my very best. That gave me hope that I was going to be okay. When I looked in the mirror I saw my mother's face, her caramel complexion, pretty dimples, and her smile. She was saying, "I'm proud of you," so I focused on my schoolwork. My mom didn't finish high school so it was important to finish with good grades. I wanted more and I was going to get it. I had hopes and dreams that were still alive in the deepest part of my existence. I had to change my outlook if I wanted to change my direction. So I pulled myself together, finished high school, worked, put myself through community college, and graduated with an Associate's degree in Accounting.

I was so proud of myself when I got a job at Princess Hotels as a reservation agent and then got an apartment. I thought I was on my way, but living over a bodega in the South Bronx was not all what I had hoped it would be. By now I was a single mother of two small sons, Jeffrey and Elijah. It wasn't a kid-friendly neighborhood, but it was all I could afford. I can still smell the waste that filled the streets, see the drug dealers on every corner, and hear the gunshots that were fired in the middle of the night. I remember jumping out of my bed in the wee hours to protect my boys out of fear of stray bullets coming through the window.

Sleep wasn't a commodity back then. My life was going to work, picking up the kids, and going home. Living behind a locked door fearing every sound the neighborhood produced; I felt like a prisoner trapped in a one bedroom box. I was miserable, unhappy, and depressed. This wasn't the life I had envisioned, but it was the one I was living. Every day my breaths were getting shorter and shorter, I was dying inside. What I was trying so hard to get away from was slowly creeping its way back. I had worked too hard to change my life and direction. I had gotten myself out of the depressed self-pity place I was in back in my youth and felt like I was living someplace I didn't feel safe; this just wasn't home. I felt trapped in that apartment, just like that little girl did when she was going from house to house trying to find someplace to call home.

I knew in my heart that things could be better I just had to make changes for it to happen. I deserved more. I couldn't sit around and accept this as my destiny, my babies deserved better. At that moment I knew I had to leave New York if I was going to survive. This place had snatched my father, stolen my mother, and I wasn't about to let it claim my life or the life of my boys.

My next move was either one of courage, fear, or insanity. You decide because my family and friends had all believed I was suffering from some kind of psychosis. I woke up one Monday morning, called in sick, took the boys to the babysitter, and took the No. 2 train to the Port Authority bus terminal. I had no idea where I was going and I didn't care. I just needed to get out of New York and I had to get out now. As I stood at the ticket counter two buses were about to leave, one to Connecticut and one to Baltimore. Since I had been to Connecticut during my high school track days, I settled on Baltimore. I knew nothing about Baltimore, had never done any research about the city so it seemed like the best choice. Something new and different was just what the occasion called for. As I boarded the bus I smiled and said to myself, "Girl, you crazy," but at that moment crazy felt good, and good was something I hadn't experienced in a long time. I was going to a city where I knew no one. I would be a stranger in a foreign land. What if someone tried to hurt me? Or worse, who would I call? Yet I was not afraid. I felt protected, and directed by the power of the Highest Authority to take this journey. I knew I would return home safely.

After a four hour ride, I stepped off the Greyhound bus in downtown Baltimore and followed the crowd down Fayette Street to Charles Street eventually reaching Pratt Street. On Pratt Street I could see the harbor and thought, *What a beautiful sight.* I continued walking, noticing all the people in their business attire heading into tall buildings that overlooked the harbor. Could this be what I've been searching for? Was this the place where my dreams would manifest? Was this home? Back then there were two pavilions that faced the harbor called Harbor View. One consisted primarily of small shops and boutiques, and the other was dedicated to food and eateries. I got something to eat and sat on a bench admiring the view. Everything looked peaceful and clean, a far cry from my current situation. Three hours passed and I didn't want to leave, but I had to get back to New York and my boys.

As I sat, I envisioned myself living there. I knew the hotel industry and there was an abundance of them downtown, so I was certain I could find employment. I felt rejuvenated, inspired, and most of all hopeful. At that moment my life changed. I had decided without a doubt to call this place my home. It would be my land of opportunity. Daydreaming about the possibilities, I lost track of time. I would be late picking up the boys, so I called my babysitter who understood and agreed to keep them until I got there. I rushed back to the bus terminal, but not before picking up a local newspaper.

On the way back to the bus I smiled at those I passed and greeted them with hellos as if they were already my neighbors. Yes, this felt right, and yes, I was excited. On the bus ride home I opened the paper to the classified section and began circling all the jobs openings I was qualified to do.

Four weeks later I had secured a job and was packing to move to Baltimore. The boys wouldn't be making the trip with me initially because I still had to secure a place for us to live. A friend of a friend named Karma allowed me to use her local address on my resumes and was gracious enough to open her door to me when I arrived. Before the boys came I would travel back to New York to spend time with them. The manager at the hotel where I worked, a mom herself, understood my situation and made every effort to give me a schedule that met my need to be with the boys. I remember leaving work on Fridays heading to the station, spending the weekend with the boys, boarding a bus early on Monday, going straight to work changing my clothes in the hotel bathroom. It was rough at times but within six weeks I was able to bring my boys to our new home. It was a modest apartment with two bedrooms, a living/dining room combination, and a small galley kitchen, nothing lavish but adequate. It was home.

Life seemed to be moving forward—a job, my boys were with me, and we had a place to live. My move was working out. I had made the right decision. Then BOOM!! While at work one day I was suddenly hit with excruciating pains in my stomach. I had been back and forth to the doctor's office about the pain previously but to no avail. This time was different. I couldn't even pick up a small trash can under my desk. My co-worker was generous enough to drive me to my doctor's office. After describing my symptoms he immediately called an ambulance and I was rushed to the hospital. My appendix had ruptured and I needed emergency surgery. Thank God one of my sisters had moved to Baltimore, at the time, and she, with the help of other family members, were able to take care of my boys. God had spared my life, Jeffery and Elijah (8 and 4) still had their mother—we were blessed. *Trouble don't last always* and it's a good thing because I had more than my fair share waiting for me when I returned home.

My employer was downsizing so I lost my job shortly after leaving the hospital. I did find another one, but it was on the other side of town and took two hours to get there on public transportation. Days were long, nights were short, but I was grateful. I was settling into this grueling routine when one evening while going through the mail I noticed a letter from the rental office. It said, "Ms. Johnson we will not be renewing your lease, you have 30 days to vacate the premises." Things were tight and the rent was late every month, but it was paid. I read the letter over and over, hoping I had misunderstood, but the words never changed. I was devastated and speechless. The next morning I ran to the leasing office pleading with them not to throw me and my family out on the streets, but my cries landed on deaf ears. What had I done? How did this happen? I was supposed to protect my children. Provide them with shelter, but I was failing. I moved here so they could have a better growing up experience and now they have no place to call home. Why did I leave New York? This is worse than living in the Bronx. I made the wrong decision; I never should have left New York.

My little pity party didn't change a thing. We had to leave. After coming to grips with the situation, I called friends and family to find someplace for us to stay. Even after all my ranting, I knew I wasn't going back to New York. I had created this mess. I had to finish what I started. What I was seeking from Baltimore was there, I just had to focus. This was my wake up call. The process of moving and finding places for my belongings was heartbreaking. It was hard to break down bunk beds to put them in storage along with our other furniture. It was clear to me at this point that I was homeless and it hurt my heart and broke my spirit. I didn't have that excited and happy feeling I had gotten when I left New York. My mission hadn't changed and I was going to have a better life. I was going to reach my goals and follow my dreams.

Bless my sister's heart; she took in the boys and me. I was angry and this wasn't what I bargained for. It wasn't fair. I had done everything to make things better and felt like I was headed in the right direction. Lying on my sister's sofa I was feeling so many emotions and believe me "blessed and highly favored" wasn't one of them. I was angry with myself, frustrated, embarrassed, defeated, and most of all I felt like I let my boys down. I was the brave sister that leaped out on faith and moved to another state, but at the moment I felt like the weakest of all of them.

As I cried myself to sleep, I asked God, "Why would you have me pick up and leave everything I had, and everyone I loved, to come here, get sick, and kicked out of my home? Do you not love me anymore? Why have you forsaken me?" But I was blessed. I had family and friends who stepped in to help. I had quickly forgotten in my moment of hurt and frustration that it was God who had brought me this far and He would carry me the rest of the way.

Looking back on it now I can see the pattern. Yes, I had made this move for the right reasons, but I had lost my focus. My environment had changed, but I hadn't. I had settled into complacency, again, going to work, picking up the kids, and going home—every day the same. I wasn't working on or towards my dreams. There was more than this out there for me, deep down I knew it. I had been brave enough to step out on faith, moving with just a paycheck in my pocket, but where had that faith gone? All I can say is that it was a temporary lapse, and from that moment I saw a future with all I had ever hoped and prayed for. I knew God was for me and with me in this and if I placed my trust, direction, and life in His hands, my dreams would manifest. I didn't know how long it would take, but I knew, I believed, I trusted He would give me the desires of my heart.

We've all heard the saying, "When God shows up, He shows out." Well, He did just that. I needed my own place. While I was grateful for my sister, my family needed more space. I knew the arrangement was temporary, but I was afraid to try again, afraid of being rejected because no one would accept me with a recent eviction on my rental history. I cried many nights over my current circumstances, but I believed within my heart, things would eventually change.

One day when a friend came to take me to an apartment complex. I went, but with some trepidation. When we pulled up, I noticed the pretty green grass and beautiful flowerbeds. The grounds were maintained expertly. There was a pool and a park the boys would absolutely love. There was even a gym filled with all types of exercise equipment. I thought, *I can get my sexy back up in here.* This was the place for me and my family, but who was I fooling, I couldn't afford this place, and they would not accept me anyway. Still, I filled out the application and gave them the required documentation then took a seat. There were two other women sitting across from the agent's desk as well. After about 20 minutes the young lady came out and said, "Ms. Johnson your application has been approved." I just sat there and looked at the other two ladies because I assumed she wasn't talking to me. Johnson is a very common name so chances were she was talking to one of them and I wasn't going to embarrass myself by getting up.

No one moved and then the lady looked directly at me and said, "Ms. Johnson." I still didn't move because I believed there was no way they would approve me after *just* getting evicted so I sat, still. Then she walk over to me and said, "Ms. Johnson, did you change your mind?" I asked if she was talking to me and she told me yes, my application was approved. I was so excited, I wanted to jump up, hug, and kiss her but I kept it inside. The boys would be excited to know they could go swimming whenever they wanted. God had given me another chance and I knew he still loved me and would always have my back. I don't know what God did, but He opened the door which the leasing agent could not shut...I WAS APPROVED! Thank you Lord!

I had been given another chance to get it right and I was going to do just that. My God deserved the best of me. He had been faithful and I was not about to disappoint Him—not again. I was focused and could see clearly for the first time in a long time. The determination I had when I decided to leave New York had returned. I vowed my rent would not be late, ever, so I took on a part-time job. I decided to go back to school, at night, to get my Bachelor's Degree in Accounting, I even decided to take a home-buyers class with the hopes of eventually buying a home.

Faith and prayer got me through this stage of my journey and I accomplished it all. In August 2005, just a few days after receiving my graduation cap and gown in the mail, I got a call from one of my realtors congratulating me, I was about to become a first time home owner. It was just shy of three years since I had moved into my new apartment. As I sat on my balcony twirling the tassel to my cap, I thought about all that I had been through to get where I was, and I realized it was all in God's Plan for me.

I believe that he always had favor over me but I was in my own way. If I had stayed at that apartment complex, would I have gotten the clear vision to go back to school and to go to homebuyer's class? I wondered if these two major milestones in my life would have come to fruition if I still lived there. I would have probably stayed at the old apartment complex if he had not stepped in and evicted me. Sometimes in life we have to let go of some places, people, and things to see and hear the path God wants us to follow. God had better things in store for me. I now realize I *had* to go through the hurt, pain, and humiliation in order to be where I am today. Sometimes you have to go through it, in order to come out of it.

Things were going well; I was in my new home, had gotten a new job, and had found love. Roger and I first meet in a supermarket back in 2000. He watched me as I was walking down the aisle and as I got closer he had no choice but to say hello. How can you look at someone walk from one end to the other, and once they reach you, not at least say hello? I thought it was cute; he was cute, and shoot, he is still very cute. I found a man who loved my boys and me, who supported me, and encouraged me to follow my heart.

I'll never forget that day in March 2013 when the man I loved so very much got on his knees and asked me to be his wife. Without hesitation I said yes because I knew he was Heaven sent. I was in a great place in my life, which opened my mind about entrepreneurship.

I began working with my husband, Roger Harris, promoting Charm City Jazz concerts. Through this venture I discovered a need that would help local entrepreneurs and benefit the business and "The Vendors Network" was born. I reached out to local vendors letting them know we were willing to find events in which they could showcase their products and services. As word of the network grew it brought with it a new challenge. I received calls from local authors asking if they could be part of the network and presents their books at some of the events. I was used to those who sold jewelry, handbags, and clothing, but not authors. As I spoke with authors I realized that it was unlikely that they would make, at the very least, their vending fee back, so in good conscious I could not accept their money, and decided to let them set up for free. The news quickly spread and my phone kept ringing from authors throughout the Maryland, DC, and Virginia areas.

There was something about the authors that weighed heavily on me. I spoke with them, often making cold calls. What I learned was that they all had the same issues, problems, and concerns. Regardless of how the conversations began they all ended with a need not being met. I had no ability to meet that need; my background was numbers not words. But I couldn't stop thinking about their plight. So I did the only thing I knew to do, I prayed. Prayer does change things and this one changed my life, yet again, but this time it was good.

God answered with, "Walk in faith." My faith walk led to the birth of "The African American Author's Expo," which is an annual event for the public to meet the people behind the stories, and the authors to showcase their artistry. Since its inception in 2009, the platform has grown from exposing independent authors to the general public to connecting them with national book clubs, organizations, and readers abroad, also offering workshops to help aspiring authors. I realized that there were young writers, as young as 10 that needed a voice, so in 2011 I created "The Youth Writer's Challenge." This program allowed youth in elementary, middle, and high school to submit their work to be judged and a winner selected. Seeing the ability of such young applicants I knew I wanted to do more and now have established The Youth Writers Challenge as a nonprofit to help these youth to enhance their talent and afford them opportunities that will secure a future in pages produced by their imaginations.

Today I know for a fact that if I had stayed in New York unhappy and depressed with the day to day demands on my life I would not have finished college, bought a home, started my own business, and married the love of my life. My sons are now thriving, independent young adults who are working diligently towards their hopes and dreams. Yes, life is good; everything I pictured has come to fruition, my cup overflows. But my greatest joy is not what I have or what I've done for my family and me although I am proud of the accomplishments of that little girl from New York. She has gotten her "happy go lucky" back.

My greatest joy lies in knowing that I have been able to make a difference in the lives of others. I'm living my best life now, and as we all know success is not a destination, it's a journey.

I want to challenge you to the following:

Step Out On Faith

If you feel that there is something you really want to do, step out on faith and not let fear or others deter you from following your dreams. You may—no, you will encounter obstacles because the devil can see what God has in store for you and will try and block your blessing. But you must keep believing in spite of and as Mary, Mary would say, "Go Get Your Blessing."

Don't Be Afraid to Fail

Failure toughens us up and makes us stronger. Almost everyone fails at their first try, the key is to not give up but try again. Remember, you have to go through it, in order to come out of it.

I know it can be hard and scary to follow your dreams. Fear, disappointment, and even failure keep many of us from walking in faith; but failure isn't fatal or final, it won't kill you, and is not the end of the world, but defeat is a choice. Trust yourself, trust in your dreams, learn from your mistakes, and they become stepping-stones to your true destiny. Those around you will question your steps, some because they want the best for you and others because they want to hold you back from receiving your blessings, but you must remember Who ordered your steps. Sometimes things will get ugly, what you envisioned won't be what you see. Dark times may get even darker. Reality will try to derail you, but you can't stay where you are. Get angry, rant, cry, or throw things if you feel the need, but get over it. Your life and future depends on it. Forgive yourself for your mistakes, pray, asking for direction and believe that God still loves you. Then the healing can begin. He's waiting to restore all you have lost; you need only to trust and believe. Defeat or victory, the choice is yours. It all depends on your next step; take the leap, walk in faith, I'm a witness that you won't regret it.

Made in the USA
San Bernardino, CA
13 May 2016